ARCHITECTURAL DIGEST CELEBRITY HOMES

Celebrity Homes

ARCHITECTURAL DIGEST PRESENTS

THE PRIVATE WORLDS OF THIRTY INTERNATIONAL PERSONALITIES

Edited by

Paige Rense

Editor-in-Chief, *Architectural Digest*

The Knapp Press   Publishers   *Los Angeles*

Published in the United States of America in 1977 by
The Knapp Press
5900 Wilshire Boulevard, Los Angeles, California 90036
Copyright © 1977 by Knapp Communications Corporation
All rights reserved
First Edition

Library of Congress Cataloging in Publication Data
Main entry under title: Architectural Digest celebrity homes
1. Interior decoration.   I. Rense, Paige.
II. Architectural digest.   III. Title: Celebrity homes
NK1980.A67   747'.8'80922   77-84047

ISBN 0-89535-001-7
Printed and bound in the U.S.A.

CONTENTS

FOREWORD

This foreword really begins in California, in 1920, when the first issue of *Architectural Digest* was published. At that time an architectural trade journal, it evolved through the years until 1965, when Cleon T. Knapp, grandson of the founder, took over and changed the editorial thrust of the magazine to interior design and directed it toward the audience of affluent consumers he believed would welcome the "new" publication.

In 1970 Mr. Knapp asked me to join the staff and give the publication more lively, informational text. In 1971 he challenged me to change the entire editorial and design content to a level of style and taste unprecedented in the United States. National magazine and newspaper articles have generously acknowledged the achievement of that goal. A series of books became our next goal. This is the first in our projected book program, to be followed with *Architectural Digest* books of American Interiors and International Interiors. Each, including, of course, this book, is composed of editorial material that appeared in the pages of *Architectural Digest* throughout the past ten years.

We selected *Celebrity Homes* for our first book because we cannot truthfully deny the influence of celebrities in our lives. Those who have achieved notability in various fields affect us in ways we may not fully realize. Film. Literature. Art. Music. The Culinary Arts. Who, watching Julia Child on television, is not curious to see her kitchen? Reading the perceptive commentary of Truman Capote and Gore Vidal prompts a certain wonderment about their personal surroundings. Who, knowing the style-making influence of French couturier Yves Saint Laurent, would not speculate about his design for private living?

We have most especially looked for those homes revealing visual clues that reflect the personalities of individual celebrities. These features, we believe—and the theory is confirmed by letters from our readers—are as interesting in five, ten or fifteen years as they are today. Fads fade, trends blur, but our preoccupation with personal style remains.

In *Architectural Digest* over the years we have featured forty-room châteaux and weekend pied-à-terres; penthouses and private railway cars; one-room apartments and seaside cottages. However, we feel that the true measure of good interior design is richness of form and imagination, atmosphere and, above all, style—that tenuous magic that draws us into the aura of the personality whose home it is, creating a memorable setting, "a continuous and stationary music," in the words of Mme. de Staël, whose own historic Château de Coppet has appeared in *Architectural Digest*. We have selected the homes of thirty outstanding personalities for this, our first book.

We found all the achievers featured here cooperative and gracious, without exception; each story a rewarding experience for all of us—editors, photographers and writers, and, we hope, for the celebrated individuals who opened their residences to us. I would like to thank them on behalf of the entire editorial staff.

Staff members and associates of *Architectural Digest* and The Knapp Press who participated in this book are mentioned on page 255. Special thanks go to Jane Jordan Browne, who edited and rewrote the original text into the proper format for this book, as well as writing new text when required; Philip Kaplan, Graphics Director for *Architectural Digest*, who conceived the format for this book and supervised every visual aspect; Margaret Redfield, who edited all copy with great sensitivity and understanding; Susan Bernard, who coordinated everything and made sure we all met our deadlines; Gayle Moss Rosenberg, who researched and wrote the captions.

There is a saying in the publishing world that there cannot be a good editor without a good publisher. So, very specially, thanks to my respected colleague and friend, President/Publisher of *Architectural Digest* and The Knapp Press, Cleon T. Knapp, who gave me the greatest gift of all—editorial freedom.

Paige Rense
Editor-in-Chief
Los Angeles, California

ARCHITECTURAL DIGEST   CELEBRITY HOMES

MERLE OBERON

Balmy weather, a breathtaking setting and an active nightlife have made Acapulco a favorite playground for the international set. Film star Merle Oberon, with her former husband Bruno Pagliai, built the first of the exotic villas that now line the cliffs and beaches of this Mexican resort. *Ghalál,* as Miss Oberon named her dramatic home-by-the-sea, means "love" in Tzotil, the ancient language of the Tula Indians. Still the showplace of the region, Ghalál has lived up to its romantic name and is a striking, distinguished local landmark.

Its situation romantically remote, on the Playa Guittarón, on the easternmost side of the bay, the five-house complex is reached by a winding private road banked with brilliant wild flowers and dense tropical growth. As the immense antique gates swing open by the gatekeeper's house, the almost savage terrain changes abruptly to a meticulously landscaped drive that slopes gently down a hillside planted with palms, ginger, brilliantly blooming bougainvillea and crape myrtle. The main house of the compound projects from the highest terrace, and an ingenious use of various levels cut into the rock dominates the rest of the structures, which seem to melt into the background of lush foliage, allowing the dramatic architecture of the main house to come forward with its full impact.

The entrance is an archway of palm trees, emulating the Moorish-inspired series of gleaming white arches that rise from a base of white Italian marble to contain the house itself. Their fluid lines carry through into the interior of the structure to create a templelike entrance hall and vaulted ceilings for the rooms within. Bronze-colored metal grilles, set into the arches, are designed with an Oriental motif, providing a decorative effect and setting the mood for the interior. They also filter the sun's brilliant rays.

Mexican architect Juan Sordo Madaleno broke with a number of traditions when he designed what he considers "the most beautiful house of my career." In Acapulco, most houses are Spanish Colonial or Bauhaus style, and certainly all avoid the hot western exposure. But Miss Oberon wanted as many rooms as possible to have a view of the spectacular Acapulco sunsets. She decided to give her home its own distinct architectural expression with the unusual use of arches. Air conditioning offsets the sun's heat and the humidity that can accompany seaside living in the tropics.

For six months bulldozers carved out the terraced site on the hillside, and the architect designed a very deep, building-length outdoor gallery facing the afternoon sun, a space that always lies partly in shade. The white roof and walls deflect the rays of the sun.

Life at Ghalál is spent outdoors as much as possible. There is no dining room, and dinner is served on the long gallery, against a backdrop of lights from the bay. Lunch is in the outdoor living room by the lagoonlike pool, from which three graceful palm trees rise, their roots protected by tile. The "room" is formed by a stone slab "floor" suspended between an upper pond and the pool, with a "roof" of palm fronds.

Merle Oberon once said, "We live outside in the brilliance of the sky and water. When I entertain four or five couples we sit under the arbor of the palms or over the bridge, with the waterfall beneath us tumbling into the sea." The waterfall is created by a jet forced through a huge boulder, part of the rugged terrain that has been carefully respected in the landscaping.

Miss Oberon had trees, vines and flowers that were growing wild in the mountains brought into the gardens near the house, to intensify the already spectacular romantic naturalism of Ghalál.

She showed the same painstaking concern for detail in designing the interiors. Tasmanian born, and raised in India, Miss Oberon created a décor that can best be called "British Colonial," a combination of comfortable English with Oriental touches. "I'm not indigenous," she remarked, "so why should Ghalál be?"

In the thirty-five-foot-square living room the major furnishings are Chinese, some original, some copies of Ming Dynasty pieces. A cabinet the length of the room holds bibelots and objets d'art, many of them rare Chinese porcelains. The cabinet also houses a stereophonic sound system that carries music throughout the house and outdoors.

The Pagliais filled their home with countless beautiful and enduring objects. Many of the pieces are extremely rare, such as the intricately carved authentic opium bed with table, in Miss Oberon's bedroom. At night it is a conventional bed; by day it is displayed as it might have been in an emperor's palace centuries ago, with the center section removed and replaced by a table. It is swathed in chiffon of deep pink, the actress's favorite color. The rugs, which she designed herself—"I don't draw very well, but I managed"—are Oriental in feeling, sprightly with bright flowers and foliage, birds and animals. The luxurious living room carpet is the famous "monkey-in-a-tree" design.

The geometry and architectural quality of the Oriental furniture, the intricate patterns and brilliant hues of the rugs and fabrics are effective counterpoints to the white and flowing Islamic architecture. Merle Oberon's vision for Ghalál has proved a work of distinction that transcends place and time.

PRECEDING PAGES AND LEFT: *A terraced hillside overlooking Acapulco Bay is the alluring site of* Ghalál, *the residence of actress Merle Oberon during her marriage to industrialist Bruno Pagliai. The main structure of the five-house complex is defined by a series of undulating Moorish arches that rise from a slab of Italian marble. Miss Oberon increased the poetic naturalism of the property by having trees, shrubs and flowers brought from the surrounding mountains into the gardens.*

BELOW AND OPPOSITE: *Miss Oberon created a "British Colonial" décor, which mixes comfortable English furnishings with Oriental pieces. The Tasmanian-born film star, reared in India, has a particular fondness for things Oriental. A cabinet stretching across the 35-foot-square Living Room is the repository for Miss Oberon's collection of English, Mexican, European and Oriental objets d'art, and for an intricate sound and lighting system serving the entire property. A Chinese-style, floral-patterned custom carpet softens the angularity of Chinese fretwork sofas and tables, and fretback English chairs. The romantic view through the glass wall of the pavilionlike room suggests the name of the house: Ghalál means "love," in Tzotil, the ancient language of the local Tula Indians.*

ABOVE: *The simple design of Mr. Pagliai's Bedroom includes a Chinese-inspired red-lacquered k'ang sofa and an Ethiopian painting that recounts the story of the Queen of Sheba. The deep arched overhang helps to control the strong light and heat.* BELOW AND RIGHT: *A distinctive chiffon-draped Chinese teak opium bed dominates Miss Oberon's pastel-toned Bedroom. During the day the center section of the mattress is removed and a low table put in its place, as it would have been in an emperor's palace. A contemporary needlepoint rug designed by Miss Oberon, and Oriental-inspired English fretwork tables and chair add to the exotic feeling.*

OPPOSITE: *Ghalál is surrounded by a wildly rugged terrain, which mellows to an oasislike fantasy inside a set of massive antique gates. The Main House rests on the highest terrace of the estate and gives the illusion of floating on the landscape. Three tile-based palm trees project dramatically from a lagoonlike pool, near the area that serves as an outdoor living room. "We live outside in the brilliance of the sky and water," Miss Oberon said of the setting.*

RIGHT: *A changing pattern of shadows cast by graceful symmetric arches plays over the white marble of the deep bayside Gallery. Most homes in the area were built to avoid the hot western exposure, but Ghalál was purposely situated so that the main rooms would face the dramatic Acapulco sunsets.*

BELOW RIGHT: *Another view of the outdoor living room shows its stone-slab floor, suspended between a pond and the swimming pool. A canopy of palm trees keeps the area in shade throughout the day. "When I entertain four or five couples we sit under the arbor of the palms or over the bridge, with the waterfall beneath us," Merle Oberon once said.*

ABOVE: *Ghalál rests like a tiara above several levels of stone retaining walls, which form terraces down to the water's edge. It took six months for bulldozers to carve the terracing on the hillside. Mexican architect Juan Sordo Madaleno has called the residence "the most beautiful house of my career."*
OPPOSITE: *Villas, hotels and resorts dot the shoreline across the bay from Ghalál's exhilarating vantage point. The residence is intentionally without a dining room; meals are served on the long gallery or at the outdoor living room, near the pool, which is studded with palm trees.*

MARY PICKFORD

Douglas Fairbanks was already courting Mary Pickford when he acquired, in 1919, a fifty-six-acre estate in the city of Beverly Hills. The Fairbankses spent their honeymoon in the hunting lodge on the property, and Miss Pickford, enchanted with the setting, decided to call on architect Wallace Neff to transform the lodge into a distinguished permanent home.

This was a time when it was not unusual to see signs reading: "No dogs, cats or motion picture actors allowed." Proudly established in her new home, Mary Pickford decided to show the world that actors knew how to live graciously.

Mr. Neff worked closely with Miss Pickford in remodeling the exteriors and interiors of the lodge, and in planning new structures. Stables were built, garages and servants' quarters added. Eighteen acres were landscaped. A few years later Mr. Neff designed a large guest wing, with two bedrooms and a sitting room. Since the lodge was "more English than anything else," it was decided to keep to this style, within as well as without.

The twenty-five-room mansion, with its sweeping lawns and Olympic-size pool, was christened *Pickfair* by the press. The residents adopted the name and engraved it on a plaque set into the marble gatepost at the driveway entrance to the property.

Screen idols and part owners of United Artists, the Fairbankses had founded a new aristocracy and their home rapidly became an institution. If Hollywood was the capital of filmdom, Pickfair was its White House, and the gracious hostess its First Lady. *Life* magazine described Pickfair as "a gathering place only slightly less important than the White House, and much more fun." The Duke and Duchess of Alba and the King and Queen of Siam were house guests. Lord and Lady Mountbatten spent their honeymoon in the guest wing. A high point of any stay would be a horseback ride at dawn to a campsite where a lavish breakfast, laid by the Pickfair staff, awaited the riders.

Hollywood's "perfect marriage" came to an end, but Pickfair's hospitality continued. Over the years, after Mary Pickford and actor/musician Charles "Buddy" Rogers were married, they expanded the traditional hospitality by opening the grounds of Pickfair for charity benefits, to as many as three thousand guests at a time.

Will Rogers once remarked, "My most important duty as the mayor of Beverly Hills is directing folks to Mary Pickford's house."

Mr. and Mrs. Rogers still reside at Pickfair, although they prefer quiet times with close friends to the gala parties of former years.

Pickfair is a durable landmark, although the environs have changed radically over the decades. Mr. Rogers remembers when guests used to saddle up and ride to the ocean, passing only one other house on the way, where the Bel-Air Hotel now stands.

The house has remained virtually unaltered, but it has been refurbished periodically under the guidance of interior designer Kathryn Crawford.

A circular drive leads to the porte cochere. Chinese red-lacquered doors open into a small entrance hall with chinoiserie wallpaper, a Chinese settee, a pair of Ming horses and niches with carved jade figurines, part of an extensive collection. A narrow stairway leads to the spacious and sunny reception hall where, in perfect symmetry, a pair of English gilt armchairs flank a painted Adam cabinet. An antique glass screen at the foot of the stairway conceals the projection room, said to be the first ever installed in a private residence. Pastel walls and polished woods, along with delicate Regency period pieces, create an atmosphere of quiet elegance. The paneled living room contains handsome Irish and Chinese Chippendale antiques.

The dining room, which Mr. Rogers considers the most perfectly proportioned room in the house, is neo-Classic in feeling. Four faceted mirrored niches with shell-motif tops hold Miss Pickford's collection of Dresden figurines and jade objects. Italian Louis XVI chairs are drawn up to a light green table of the same style. The guest wing is paneled in pine and furnished with English and French antiques, including a unique pair of painted tester beds. French doors open to a formal Italian garden.

Traditional Pickfair is full of dramatic surprises. At the porte cochere level is the Western bar, a perfect Hollywood setting. Rough stucco walls are decorated with paintings and sculpture by Frederic Remington. The twelve-foot-long solid mahogany bar, originally brought around the Horn, was once the center of attraction in McGuire's Union Saloon, in Auburn, California. An old desk once served as a post office. "It stood on the grass in front of the grain store in Olathe, Kansas, my hometown," Mr. Rogers recalls.

On the fourth floor are the famous Oriental rooms, which serve as a museum for the gifts showered on the Fairbankses when they visited the Orient. Here, too, are costumes worn by Miss Pickford in many of her memorable motion picture roles.

Pickfair, her home for almost six decades, has fully realized Mary Pickford's original intent to create a lasting impression of gracious living. In her own words, it is "a luxurious, dignified and comfortable American home, retaining its reputation and status through the years, in spite of the many passing fads."

OPPOSITE: *The garden façade of Pickfair, one of the most fabled of Beverly Hills estates, bespeaks the tranquil dignity its renowned residents desire; now Mary Pickford and her husband, Buddy Rogers, prefer quiet times with close friends. In past decades the twenty-five-room mansion served as an elegant gathering place for the most glamorous members of Hollywood aristocracy. Acquired by Douglas Fairbanks in 1919 for his bride, Mary Pickford, the rustic hunting lodge—surrounded by fifty-six wooded hillside acres—was remodeled by Wallace Neff as a formal English manor.*

ABOVE: *The sunny Reception Hall looks out over a sloping lawn. Architectural details are neo-Classic and the appointments are traditional. The parquetry floor is polished mahogany laid in a hexagonal pattern. Oval figure paintings and flower garlands decorate a shaped-front Adam cabinet, while a pastoral panel enhances the Louis XVI trumeau. An English gilt armchair is one of a pair flanking the cabinet; above the chairs are small French paintings.*

RIGHT: *The imposing 45-foot-long Living Room is paneled in wiped wood to blend with an Adam mantel. Contemporary sofas mix with rich antique mahogany pieces and Oriental objets d'art. Over the mantel is a portrait of Mary Pickford by Portuguese artist Henrique Medina.*

BELOW: *An arrangement in one corner of the Living Room includes a pair of medallion-fret Chinese Chippendale chairs, an Irish Chippendale kettle-base chest and a chinoiserie vitrine mirror. Porcelain and jade objects, part of an extensive collection, accessorize many of the rooms.*

LEFT: *The pastel-toned Dining Room expresses a soft formality. Italian Louis XVI furnishings retain the mellow patina of their original paint and gilding. In the background is one of four faceted mirrored niches that hold Dresden figurines and jade objects. A Romney portrait hangs above the sideboard.*

ABOVE: *The Breakfast Room's large bay window extends the space to include a lush garden landscape. Eighteenth-century Venetian furniture reflects Louis XVI styling. The feathered occupants of a lovely antique bird cage seem to exult in their sun-warmed vantage point. Daisies from the garden, upheld by porcelain cherubs, freshen the room.*

31

The large Guest Wing has offered lavish hospitality to visiting royalty and film celebrities for half a century; Lord and Lady Mountbatten spent their honeymoon here. Horseback rides at dawn and elegant picnic breakfasts were de rigueur.
ABOVE: The pine-paneled Sitting Room separates two guest bedrooms. Architectural details harmonize with antique French and English furniture and an intricately carved Georgian Rococo mirror above the mantel. The painting is by G. Seignac.
RIGHT: Delicate late-eighteenth-century Hepplewhite furniture, in a combination of colored woods and painted decoration, distinguishes a Guest Bedroom.
OPPOSITE: From the second floor of the main house, Mr. and Mrs. Rogers enjoy a splendid view of the parterred formal Italian Garden, which edges the brick terrace of the guest wing.

CECIL BEATON

On August 15, 1924, a young Cecil Beaton wrote in his diary his reaction to Norwich Cathedral: "I should like to have a room at Cambridge built exactly like some of the hidden apses and chapels. It would be a long massive room. All whitewashed stone with enormous arches and one or two theatrical but simple pieces of dull gold furniture. A huge fire could burn at one end of the room. A gold dining table at the other might have a cloth of gold on it, with gold plate and red gladioli in tall vases. I would have people come to lunch, just so I could terrify and impress them."

As a mature artist, his continued fascination with décor is a hallmark of Cecil Beaton's public, as well as private, life. He has two homes, one in the country and one in town, each very different, and distinguished by his remarkable artistic talent.

"Perhaps," he once wrote, "to have a house in London and another in the country is a great extravagance. However, since I am like a juggler spinning plates in the air, and trying to carry on simultaneously four or five different professions, it would be almost impossible to operate from under one roof."

The public Cecil Beaton is author, painter, photographer, set designer and costume designer. The private man is a gardener, art collector, arbiter of taste, and host to some of the most brilliant members of English society. The settings he has created for his many-textured life are in dramatic contrast.

The London townhouse is headquarters for a fast-paced city life—a schedule of appointments and conferences, theater, ballet, opera and concerts. His country place is where Mr. Beaton can work without interruption, garden at leisure and entertain his friends occasionally.

Reddish House is in Broad Chalke, Wiltshire, not far from the cathedral town of Salisbury. A classic Charles II structure built in 1662, it is considered one of the great small houses of England, an architectural jewel in an impeccable setting of formal manor gardens and thatched cottages. Essayist Lord David Cecil, Mr. Beaton's friend and neighbor, has called it a "vest-pocket edition of a three-volume novel." Three centuries of existence in the peaceful Sussex countryside have mellowed its brick and stone façade to a soft lilac hue.

Mr. Beaton took the formality of the façade, with its stone pilasters and the niche above the door pediment, as a point of departure for his decoration of the interior. "The house seems to demand a certain respect," he feels.

Classically proportioned within as well as without, the rooms of Reddish House are spacious but not cavernous. The elegance of the architectural details, such as the marble Corinthian columns and the carved moldings, is enhanced by period furnishings. Most of the wallpapers are period replicas and the rugs are formally patterned Aubussons. The furniture, all of an extraordinary quality, is a mixture of styles and periods against a background rich in color and pattern.

In Mr. Beaton's words, "The house has evolved into something essentially English in character, in spite of the fact that the furniture is mainly period French and Chinese. It is filled with far too many flowers, with old rose chintzes, Regency carpets, astrolabes, folding library steps, and everywhere a jumble of books and beloved objects picked up on my journeys abroad."

The famed art collection reflects Cecil Beaton's wide-ranging taste. Here in ideal harmony are Victorian still lifes, early Dalis, a vase by Picasso, the best of the Impressionists, eighteenth-century equestrian prints and a Renaissance madonna.

"The life I lead in each house really dictates its decoration," Mr. Beaton observes. In the country, where he researches, designs and writes, there are desks and bookcases and art folios. Chairs and sofas are large and comfortable, a natural, inviting place for relaxed conversation and listening to music.

The beautifully manicured gardens are tended by Mr. Beaton himself, with a typical Englishman's passion for growing things. A favorite spot is the "winter garden," an elegant and cheerful conservatory for year-round gardening, with a pool and fountain.

While Reddish House has the ease of a commodious English country house with cozy dress-for-dinner décor, Mr. Beaton's London townhouse represents a complete change of pace. The small Regency house in South Kensington is realized in a spare style, with bold splashes of color and an Oriental sobriety. When he took over the house, his mother having moved away from London, Mr. Beaton enlarged rooms and windows to give an illusion of space. His goal was to simplify, to make the house look contemporary and, at the same time, individual. The solution was to design many of the pieces himself, including the brass-and-steel bed in his room; to commission others, such as the chairs, tables and lamps by Diego Giacometti, and to use in a special way objects and textiles he had chosen on trips abroad. Cushions are covered with geishas' obis, and black velvet walls set off primitive masks and modern art. "It is the combination, and not the collection, which is significant," he says.

"My country place is in contrast to my townhouse," he points out, "and contrasts are always stimulating. Although the environment may become familiar, the constant change from one house to the other enhances one's sense of being alive each day of the week."

OPPOSITE: Reddish House, *in Broad Chalke, Wiltshire, near the cathedral town of Salisbury, is the country home of Cecil Beaton. The stone-pilastered brick façade of the Charles II structure, built in 1662, has mellowed over the centuries to a soft lilac hue. Over the pediment is a bust of a Roman poet.*

Lord David Cecil calls this architectural gem "a vest-pocket edition of a three-volume novel." Here Mr. Beaton finds a change of pace from his London life: "Near me in Wiltshire there are several households where talk is as good as is to be heard in a university college. Country people often possess a philosophy that is difficult to cultivate in the stress of town life."

ABOVE: *Another view of the exterior of Reddish House shows the "winter garden" conservatory wing, the smooth greensward and part of the topiary. When he returns to London Mr. Beaton takes with him baskets of just-picked salad greens, vegetables and fresh flowers, especially his favorite lilies, "a bundle of flowers unlike those you buy at the florist. The English, perhaps better than most, know how to live comfortably," he comments. "And, in spite of what you may have heard, they prefer warm rooms. Reddish House is really where I live and where I paint, design and write. Like the farmer, I come to London to do my marketing and to take further orders, but it is here in the country at Reddish that much of the real job is done."*

The interior design of the Drawing Room respects the classical architecture of Reddish House, while dark walls give contrast to its light columns and niches. The Aubusson carpet and Louis XV and XVI furniture add a continental dimension. In front of the window at the curved end wall stands a tall inlaid Louis XVI desk with gilt bronze mounts. Meissen jars in recessed niches hold fruit blossoms, and a guéridon displays a Sèvres porcelain-and-ormolu urn. Sharing the draped table with fresh garden flowers is a drawing of Cecil Beaton by the English artist Augustus John.

"The house has evolved into something essentially English in character," Mr. Beaton notes, "in spite of the fact that the furniture is mainly period French and Chinese. It is filled with far too many flowers, with old rose chintzes, Regency carpets, astrolabes, folding library steps, and everywhere a jumble of books and objects picked up on my journeys abroad."

LEFT: *A view of the Entrance Hall reveals the elegant architectural details of Reddish House: marble columns, dentil cornices and a delicate iron stair rail. In the large hall, which is also used as a dining room, a Picasso vase, filled with freshly picked lilies from the garden, stands on a marble-topped Empire table.*

OPPOSITE: *Mr. Beaton maintains a perpetual spring in his buoyant "Winter Garden" conservatory. This room was added several years after the designer acquired his country estate, so that he could indulge in his year-round hobby of gardening. A goldfish pool, set into the tile floor, and the delicate blues and whites of the vases, jardinieres and banquettes conjure up the fantasy of a Chinese porcelain willow scene. Scarlet geraniums interject a note of verisimilitude, though the blues and lavenders of other flowers reintroduce the dreamlike quality of an English "golden afternoon." The Gothic arches of numerous windows frame vistas of the grounds, replete with thatched cottages and a woodland of beeches, oaks and sycamores to complete the pastoral beauty.*

ABOVE LEFT AND ABOVE: *Two aspects of the Library indicate its versatility as a small sitting room as well as a working study. Mr. Beaton keeps his research materials in the country, where he concentrates on designing and writing. Book-lined niches flank the inlaid marble mantel. The handsome fruitwood desk once belonged to Lady Juliet Duff.*

JAMES GALANOS

When he first established himself as a fashion designer, James Galanos acquired a small house in West Hollywood. Several times winner of the prestigious American Fashion Critics Award, he is a member of their Hall of Fame. In succeeding years he has been collecting not only accolades but period furnishings and handsome art objects as well.

A perfectionist in all things, Mr. Galanos pays as much attention to detail in his home as in his celebrated fashion designs. With a true designer's eye, he always insists on the finest materials and the best execution.

"Anyone involved in the arts uses his sensibility of line and color in everything he does," says Mr. Galanos, explaining why he chose to design his home himself, relying on his own unerring sense of style. An artist whose touchstone is originality, Mr. Galanos finds uniformity singularly uninteresting. His house is a true Galanos original, and the designer's signature is evident. "I have very definite ideas," he adds. "I love antiques, fabrics and planning.

"Mine is a perfect bachelor house," he comments. "It is very suitable for me because I don't bring work home and I rarely entertain here."

The house is more or less as it was when he bought it. The library, however, was very small, so he added to it, about six feet—"as much as I could manage without upsetting the courtyard.

"What I did was to refine the doors, the woodwork, the paneling. I stained some floors dark, to make them dramatic, and I like the way the Greek rug picks up the colors of the house."

The somber elegant look of the décor is reminiscent of Mr. Galanos' dramatic creations, its drama heightened by a "midnight" lighting effect specified by the designer, who likes "living in the dark." The dark red velvets and brocades of the living room look deep and rich in the soothing half-light. "I like a quiet atmosphere," he explains, "and I need a retreat after the long intense hours in the world of fashion."

Mr. Galanos' retreat is another world, a world redolent of the eighteenth century with its combination of opulence and classic simplicity of line. He prefers formality and precision. Relationships of object to object and person to person are carefully defined. In the living room, guests are seated on matching Louis XVI canapés near tables of a Galanos design. The designer has arranged a number of diverse clean-lined objects in a new geometry that is fluid yet totally precise.

The words restraint, simplicity, quality punctuate James Galanos' conversation. "In fashion I repeatedly simplify. Embellishment is something so many overdo in fashion and in interior design. A dress can be very intricate and very detailed, but the overall look is simple. The details are there, but they don't shout at you." In furnishings he likes anything simplified, from any period. As an example of "something with very simple lines," he points to an elegant backgammon table with a marquetry surface and slim tapered legs.

Although Mr. Galanos insists that he is not wedded to any particular period, many of the pieces are of the eighteenth century: a Dutch burl commode; an Italian Baroque mirror on the wall of the small dining room; a pair of crystal girandoles by the living room fireplace. A Trojan head is a copy from the Neo-classical era. Each piece is arranged for proportion and balance, yet the effect is unstudied. "A little clutter, but not too much, is what I strive for," the designer remarks with the hint of a smile. "The cluttered look can be all right, but it is important to know when to stop."

A collector with particular taste, he acquires only works of quality. "I have no patience for sorting out from many things," he explains. "I would rather seek the best from a gallery or an antiques shop with a reputation for reliability and authenticity." For him, a signature does not mean anything of itself; a signed piece and a reproduction are judged by the same aesthetic standards. "I collect anything to do with the arts," he continues, "paintings, sculpture, books. If you don't buy something when you see it, you lose the opportunity. Whenever I see something I really like, I take it, whether I have a need for it at that moment or not. I just put it aside, and when the occasion calls, I switch. No matter how beautiful the piece or how lovely the workmanship, there must be a place for it, and it must be the right place."

A custom-designed bed in the style of Louis XV dominates the bedroom, which, like the rest of the house, is dramatic and dark. Heavy black and brown patterned Belgian velour covers the bed, drapes the headboard and warms the walls. A Chinese hard-stone screen further diminishes the amount of daylight reaching the room through shuttered windows.

"My personal preference, obviously," says the noted designer, "is for the dark and elegant. But I would say I am open to all décor."

An adjacent dressing room and bath carry out the color theme with black-lacquered ceiling and brown marble appointments. "Very simple," Mr. Galanos notes, "and tailored for a man.

"I simplify, simplify, simplify," he adds. "My house is deliberately small. I keep it as my retreat, and it is, in essence, another world to me. You see, I'm trying to live in the eighteenth century."

James Galanos' compact West Hollywood residence has a marked similarity to the fashion designs for which he is internationally celebrated; in both, dark colors are used, to dramatic elegant effect.

LEFT: *A wall of antiqued mirror and a deeply colored velvet-draped bay in the Living Room help to achieve Mr. Galanos' desired "midnight" lighting. The surface of the wall at right is varied by a paneled screen with mounted sconces. An eighteenth-century Dutch burl commode, displaying two Chinese* **famille verte** *vases and a Neo-classical head, stands in front of the screen. Two Galanos-designed tables serve the main conversation groupings, which consist of two late-eighteenth-century French canapés covered in rich brocade, a pair of Louis XV fauteuils covered in a gold fabric, and two small Louis XVI fauteuils. A pair of shaped Venetian oils after the manner of Guardi are mounted on the mirrored wall. The handwoven Byzantine-patterned rug is Greek.*

ABOVE: *A small painting by William Brown adorns the piano in the Living Room. Antiquities include a T'ang head and a Tanagra head, a small Greek terra-cotta figurine and an Attic bowl with figures.*

LEFT: *In a dimly lit corner of the Living Room the somber tones of a tablescape are echoed in a small painting by Thomas Keogh, titled* Five Seated Figures.

BELOW: *The matte finish of a vivid wall fabric contrasts with the shiny hard surface of a mirrored Living Room fireplace alcove. The smoky mirrored area reflects without brightness and displays a Louis XVI barometer. French carved wooden doors, painted and gilded, are mounted on the sides of the alcove, and two crystal girandoles flank the fireplace. In the corner at left is a framed Chinese fragment.*

OPPOSITE: *Two small screens and a cushion with a Japanese crest add Oriental motifs to the velvet-upholstered Library. The lacquered Chinese table displays inkwells and an obelisk, both from Mr. Galanos' crystal collection. The cushions on small folding seats are covered in a brocade fabric used in one of the designer's fashion collections.*

RIGHT: *Unusual dark marble in the Bathroom has butterfly-matched veining.*

BELOW: *A custom-made Louis XV-style bed in a specially designed space dominates the Bedroom; all paneling and architectural detailing throughout the one-bedroom house are handcarved. Bed and walls are covered in a heavy Belgian velour. The Directoire* bureau plat *holds crystal objects, Egyptian sculpture and a Louis XVI candelabrum made into a lamp. A Chinese screen in front of shuttered windows is decorated with luminous jade and coral.*

OPPOSITE: *A view of the Dressing Room from the Bedroom reveals a fruitwood armoire and more of the same velour pattern on walls and daybed. A small icon and two French carriage clocks appear on bookshelves framing the doorway. Neo-classical garniture made into a lamp stands on the marquetry bedside table.*

EARL BLACKWELL

It is said that a celebrity is a person who requires no further identification beyond the name. Earl Blackwell's Celebrity Service is for the famous and those who want to know where the famous are located at any given moment. Subscribers include the White House, television networks, numerous fund-raising organizations, multinational corporations and the FBI.

"It all started," says Earl Blackwell, "because I like people of accomplishment. In fact, I've made knowing them my life's work."

With a unique talent and a rented typewriter, he packaged an idea into an international business. His master files, begun in 1939 and now numbering over 100,000 names, are presided over by a large staff at the headquarters in New York, with branch offices in Hollywood, London, Paris and Rome.

There is a story that Tallulah Bankhead once asked him to find an apartment for her. Mr. Blackwell retorted that he "didn't do that sort of thing." "You call yourself Celebrity Service?" Miss Bankhead rejoined. "Well, I'm a celebrity and I demand service." She got her apartment.

Social arbiter and host on a grand scale, Mr. Blackwell plans to perfection events attended in force by international society. Such occasions often benefit an important charity and sometimes celebrate events of historical importance. The pace is fast and exciting but Mr. Blackwell has his own way of finding peace and quiet. Usually he flies every other weekend to his second home, in the Bahamas. "I love New York," he says, "but I have to get away." Once a month he returns to Atlanta, where he shares with his sister and her family an eight-bedroom carriage house built at the turn of the century.

Earl Blackwell's penthouse apartment on New York's West Side is surrounded by a terrace planted with gnarled catalpa and sturdy Japanese maple trees. "I love the location, opposite Carnegie Hall, and the view from the terrace," he says. The view down Fifty-seventh Street is spectacular, from river to river.

The décor is opulent, reminiscent of the Venetian palaces Mr. Blackwell so admires. In Venice, in 1967, he masterminded a masked ball in Palazzo Tezzonico that has been called "one of the parties of the century."

The furnishings of his apartment are, for the most part, Chinese and Italian. An eight-panel cinnabar screen stands behind a comfortable sofa and Chinese table in one sitting room. The rugs are family heirlooms. The colors of the screen, rugs and pillowed sofa, subdued variations of Chinese red and bright blue, are repeated in red-lacquered tables, a Venetian glass dish, a Chinese vase and a group of dancing figures found in Venice.

For seven summers Mr. Blackwell cruised the Mediterranean as a guest of Mr. and Mrs. Charles Revson on their yacht, and many art objects in the apartment are mementos of his travels. On a skirted table, an alabaster vase lamp and Oriental figures and porcelains are arranged artistically with a venerable icon from a Greek island. The backdrop is an ancient Siamese wall hanging, found in Bangkok. The multilayered sweetmeat container on the table was found in China, during his first trip around the world.

It is the justly famous private ballroom, "one of the few left in New York City," notes Mr. Blackwell, that is the center of hospitality for his large parties. Here he brings together people of the arts and theater, society, sports and politics. Through a screen of catalpa leaves three large windows illuminate the elegant room with its polished parquet floors, painted chairs, and walls decorated with murals in the Venetian style. "I wanted the ballroom to look very old," Mr. Blackwell explains, "so William Hankinson painted some trompe l'oeil cracks on his murals. After all these years, some of the walls have started to really crack. I thought of having the artist come in and restore the murals, but most of my friends say, 'Let them age as if they've been there for centuries.' And I have come to agree with them.

"The ballroom opens up beautifully," he continues. "When I have a dinner party, I use two tables for eight and one for ten, in the dining room. Afterward, I may have seventy-five more guests for drinks and dancing. In June, when I have my annual party, guests can wander around the entire terrace, to the dining room and ballroom and back again."

The little gold chairs, acquired at auction, are from the Vanderbilt home in Philadelphia. Mr. Blackwell bought the Steinway piano for Noël Coward's use when the composer was renting his apartment on Fifty-fourth Street. "It is a special souvenir," Mr. Blackwell comments. "Noël selected it and played it often."

A consummate host, Mr. Blackwell wants his guests to feel welcome the moment they arrive. "I think lots of effort should be made at the entrance in every way possible. I always have flowers, usually pink carnations and pink and red roses, to give my guests a lift the moment they step inside the door. The most important thing is to plan every detail beforehand. Then relax. If you aren't relaxed, your guests won't be.

"Sometimes an elaborate room with lots of color becomes boring over the years, but the ballroom is a beautiful room, and I've never grown tired of it."

In this setting of enduring beauty, Earl Blackwell has shared his pleasures and interests with many of the most distinguished and talented people in the world.

Earl Blackwell has often been described as "the celebrity's celebrity." His
Celebrity Register is justly famous, as are his roles of social arbiter
and party planner. His terraced Westside New York penthouse
apartment is surrounded by catalpa and Japanese maple trees. "I love the
location, opposite Carnegie Hall, and the view from the terrace," he says.
OPPOSITE: Objects on a skirted table offer clues to Mr. Blackwell's
opulent design theme: An Italian alabaster lamp sheds soft light on a
Greek icon, an Imari dish with cup and saucer, a tiered porcelain
sweetmeat container, Cambodian bronzes and a Nepalese gilt bronze. The
Chinese dog was a gift from Merle Oberon. A pierced pottery garden
pedestal supports a venerable Chinese figure, providing an interesting
counterpoint to the Siamese wall hanging.
ABOVE: Euterpe, the Greek Muse of music, dominates a trompe l'oeil
niche in the Italianate Entrance Hall. Venetian sconces, a Rococo table
beneath the painted niche, and four Italian Directoire chairs complete the
Mediterranean mood. According to Mr. Blackwell, "Everything was
gathered very carefully over a period of years."

BELOW: *A personal collection of portraits and photographs attests to Mr. Blackwell's reputation as confidant of the celebrated, including, from left to right, Serge Obolensky, the Duchess of Kent, Noël Coward, Elizabeth Taylor and Richard Burton, Francis Cardinal Spellman, and Princess Chichibu of Japan. Of his parties he says: "I like to mix people of the arts with those in the theater and society, sports and politics; and I like to mix ages. If you invite just one little set they'll be bored, because they're always with the same people."*

OPPOSITE: *The ruddy tones of a comfortable sofa and large pillows in Mr. Blackwell's private Sitting Room are complemented by a fine cinnabar screen. Japanese lacquered tables flanking the sofa add an interesting note of Oriental formality, while the coloring of a pair of heirloom Chinese rugs interposes a cooling influence. The low Chinese table with a fretwork apron holds a number of keepsakes: The nineteenth-century Staffordshire figure of a greyhound casually ignores a trio of Chinese musician figures and a pair of silver fighting cocks. "Everything in this room was brought exactly as it was, from my apartment on Fifty-fourth Street," Mr. Blackwell comments. "That was in 1959."*

A 30-by-40-foot Ballroom is a considerable help to a man noted for the elegance of his parties. The polished herringbone-patterned parquet floor, the murals, in the Venetian manner, and Directoire-style tables, stools and chairs give the room a mellow quality. "I wanted it to look very old," Mr. Blackwell explains, "so William Hankinson painted some trompe l'oeil cracks on his murals." The Steinway piano was bought for Noël Coward's use when the composer was renting Mr. Blackwell's former apartment: "Noël selected it and played it often during the three months when I was in Europe."

WOODY ALLEN

Woody Allen, writer, comedian, actor, producer, director and jazz musician, is a master at projecting the public personality he wants on view. His Manhattan home reveals the private man. The two selves are radically different. "I am nothing like I am in films, and not at all what you think I am," Mr. Allen warns. The private man is almost grave, concerned with the meaning of life; a reader of Kierkegaard and a collector of Kokoschka.

Anyone exposed to Mr. Allen's celebrity image would expect his residence to be contemporary, offbeat, even defiantly avant-garde. But the ambience of his duplex penthouse is traditional, and the mood mellow. In a typical seriocomic aside, he once told *The New Yorker*, "I think I can say, though this is not for publication, that I have the most beautiful apartment in New York."

A devoted Manhattanite who needs space and privacy, Mr. Allen chose the penthouse setting for spaciousness and the spectacular view. The lower level of the apartment, where he works and entertains, is surrounded by a narrow terrace filled with flowering plants. The large upper terrace, wrapping around the master bedroom and dressing room, is a small park of trees and plantings and a small pond. Interior woods and quiet colors deliberately play into the landscaping, creating an experience in light and shadow. At some points greenery envelops everything except the tip of a distant skyscraper.

The duplex was restructured to provide the required privacy and to expand the space. On the lower floor two adjoining apartments were merged to give access to the terraces surrounding both areas. Window openings were small and spotted erratically throughout the apartment, blocking sweeping views of park and sky. To correct this, external walls were opened and floor-to-ceiling solar glass was installed, presenting four-directional vistas of Central Park and Manhattan, and creating a floating unconfined feeling.

In the elevator foyer the main entry door, leading to the rear apartment, was blocked to create a private foyer. Common walls of the two apartments were knocked down and partitions razed between the original rooms: foyer and living room, kitchen, servants' quarters and two tiny bedrooms.

Although interior designer Olga San Giuliano had done another apartment for Mr. Allen seven years before, utilizing silk walls and Aubusson rugs, she realized that his taste had changed. The new apartment was to be Mr. Allen's present vision of himself, conceptualized in terms of design.

Olga San Giuliano approaches design as a sculptor would a lump of clay. To her, a room is an armature; she builds from the bones out, then fleshes in. And instead of carrying the clean-cut architectural lines into contemporary furnishings, the direction was toward warmth and informality. The design evolved from furniture and objets d'art that Mr. Allen had chosen over the years, from classic Jacobean to rustic French; from old masters to the German Expressionists. The result is an undecorated look of tasteful guidance, rather than of things marshaled forth to announce an effect.

Color is critical in the San Giuliano scheme of things; the designer uses it to express the theme of a room. "First," she explains, "the mood is determined—elegant, austere or intimate. Then I work out a color palette to express that ambience. Psychological tests show that certain colors can affect people's sense of space and time. Colors can make an object appear weightier or lighter, recede or advance. Color becomes an instrument."

The color theme in Mr. Allen's apartment is one of serenity and harmony with nature. "Earth tones were used," Miss Giuliano explains, "ranging from beiges and browns to russets and the rosy mauves suggested by New York sunsets. Wherever blues and reds were introduced, as in the master bedroom, the shades were soft. For example, the background of the bedroom floor is a red that seems to have been weathered for years."

To create a feeling of rusticity and spontaneity, the painted floor was stenciled in a design of crudely drawn scattered sprays of flowers. The dining room floor was painted and stenciled in a trellis acorn pattern; the designer also made use of Oriental rugs throughout the house. Hamadans, Soumaks and Turkomans are used for upholstery, as pillow covers, mirror frames and floor coverings. "The rugs have that special mellowness that comes with age," the designer points out. "They are interesting art forms in themselves, and here they become immediate visual and tactile experiences."

Miss San Giuliano is as strongly critical of the designer who acts out his own fantasies at the client's expense as she is committed to working with the fantasies and inner life of her clients. She describes her experiences with Mr. Allen: "The fantasies are acted out on the screen. He is a knowledgeable, serious man, without flash, but with an extraordinarily correct eye. I worked to understand the whole person; then I expressed who he is privately."

Mr. Allen once remarked, "My only regret in life is that I'm not someone else." Maybe he is. Judith Viorst, who was invited to an elegant dinner *à deux* with Mr. Allen, wrote: "He lives in this spectacular upper Fifth Avenue full-fledged penthouse with a knockout view of the skyline of New York, and furnishings so quietly, classily, knowingly elegant that the person who owns them ought to be Cary Grant."

*First-time visitors to Woody Allen's
Manhattan penthouse are sometimes
surprised by this reflection of his private,
rather than public, personality. The duplex,
overlooking Central Park, is a comfortable
and understated home for a serious man
whose career has been built on making
people laugh. New York designer and
teacher Olga San Giuliano designed an
earlier, more flamboyant apartment for
Mr. Allen, and she notes that his taste has
changed: "He is a knowledgeable, serious
man, without flash, but with an
extraordinarily correct eye."*
RIGHT: *A rare sight in Manhattan, a
large rooftop country garden with a rustic
pond, lush trees and plantings.*

ABOVE: *Floor-to-ceiling solar glass replaced exterior walls, allowing breathtaking views of New York on all sides. In the Living Room, the Colonial mantel is edged with Delft tile. The main seating area is composed of a large sofa covered in antique velvet, a love seat, and two lounge chairs in French frisé. A Windsor chair stands in the foreground. Table lamps were converted from old containers. Plants in Indian baskets rest on an early-nineteenth-century Swiss painted chest in the foreground. The column-front chest near the window is also Swiss.*
LEFT: *A mirror framed in an intricately patterned Oriental rug fabric is located near the Hall.*

OPPOSITE: *Stenciled floors in the sunny Dining Room provide an unusual decorative background for an antique French butcher's table surrounded by custom chairs with exposed rush seats. The Welsh dresser, flanked by a pair of wing chairs, displays a collection of patterned English earthenware plates.*

LEFT: *In the Master Bedroom, printed linen draperies and matching spread with canopy comprise the main pattern in the room. Floors stenciled in a design of scattered nosegays, white linen wall upholstery, an English four-poster bed and a pair of Swiss tavern chairs form an interesting combination of styles.*

BELOW: *In the Library, a custom-designed bench upholstered with a Turkoman rug is an innovative component of the design. Eighteenth-century Spanish chairs, studded with nailheads, an English leather sofa, and a low table, converted from an old desk, add to the contemplative mood; overmantel sconces are old railroad fixtures. Mr. Allen sometimes writes at the time-mellowed Spanish refectory table in the foreground.*

COCO CHANEL

No one can honestly claim to have known Coco Chanel. There are rooms in her life that no one ever entered. Her world was compartmentalized in a way that no one can fathom; even her home was divided. The apartment where she dined, talked, entertained, often worked and sometimes napped, is on the third floor of the House of Chanel, 31 rue Cambon. It was there she lived.

At day's end, with nothing left to do, Chanel would walk down the famous mirrored staircase, through the formal glitter of her salon, and cross the street to the Ritz Hotel to sleep. It was there she died.

"The Ritz apartment was nothing, compared to rue Cambon. It was colorless, nondescript," writes Marcel Haedrich in his book *Coco Chanel: Her Life, Her Secrets.* At her death all of Chanel disappeared from the Ritz, even the traces of the Chanel perfume she was never without.

Chanel's apartment in the House of Chanel is another story. Here one enters a museum, a shrine of great beauty, but no more and no less so than during her lifetime. Chanel is dead; Chanel lives. If Chanel, flanked by her great Venetian blackamoors, were standing at the mirrored door in the many-mirrored entrance, Chanel and Chanel and Chanel would be reflected a dozen times, symbolizing the effect of her legend during her life.

Marcel Haedrich recalls his impressions when he first visited the great fashion designer: "I was in Ali Baba's cave with treasures of Golconda: calamander [Coromandel] screens, mother-of-pearl, ebony, ivory, deer and lions, gold and crystal, masks, rare books, spheres, magic, the scent of tuberoses. It was Byzantium and the imperial palace of China, Ptolemy's Egypt, and, in the mirrors above the fireplace, reflections of Greece, with a fourth-century Aphrodite side by side with a raging wild boar, a meteorite that had fallen from the sky on Mongolia thousands of years ago, everything agglomerated and conglomerated, mingled and mangled, ordered into a disorder made harmonious by Coco's taste."

"Those on whom legends are built are their legends," Chanel once said. The legend of Chanel lives. "Never a day goes by that I don't find myself quoting Chanel," says Hervé Mille, a distinguished Paris publisher and perhaps Chanel's closest friend.

Mirrors; mirrors on mirrors. A pair of Chinese deer, the famous doeskin-covered sofa, lions—her astrological sign was Leo—heavy crystal chandeliers reflected to infinity, tables in front of tables—who but Chanel would place eleven tables in one small living room? Glitter and gold, tiny rooms filled with massive objects, against a background of monotones, the essence of Chanel.

She was both inimitable and widely copied, and, as in fashion and jewelry, Chanel's mark in decoration is still remarkably significant.

If she had an influence beyond her own instinctive good taste, it came from M. Mille's brother, Gérard Mille, one of the best-known interior designers in Paris.

"Gérard did help her," Hervé Mille concedes, "but it was mutual. She said he was the greatest influence on her, and he said she was the greatest influence on him.

"Chanel invented the use of reversed calfskin," remarks M. Mille in his own apartment, pointing to a sofa covered in black. "Her idea was to open perspective with mirrors and to favor big, even outsized, pieces. She was the first person to put huge pieces in a small room, and defy the conventional wisdom."

Cecil Beaton says of Chanel's fashion designs, in *The Glass of Fashion*, "She had an unerring sense of colour, emphasizing the use of black, which she considered extremely chic, and of white, but eschewing bright colours except in combination with a bold shade that would have a restraining effect. Pastel fashions, she said, were only for red-headed women."

"Fashion passes, style remains," Chanel once said. Her apartment is a monument to her own uniqueness. Objects from everywhere—all put together with matchless flair. A splendid ornate Louis XV wall clock by Caffiéri, backed by a plain mirror, is suspended over an eighteenth-century desk. "Some people think luxury is the contrary of being poor," Chanel once said in her terse aphoristic style. "It is not. It is the contrary of vulgarity."

She liked gold so much that if she bought a silver box she would have it dipped in gold. It was the color she liked, not the value.

Chanel's dining room walls are covered with a textured wheat-colored fabric; the curtains are beige silk. In the living room the curtains are jute, a tobacco color, and the walls are jute lacquered with gold. Color comes from the objects: gold, vermeil from the Duke of Westminster, crystal, glitter, rose quartz, flowers.

Except for a small work by Dali, a stalk of wheat, there are no paintings. "She never had paintings, never collected paintings," says Mille. "She once had one of the early Renoirs and Rousseau's *The Sleeping Gypsy*.

"She was a connoisseur by intuition," Hervé Mille recalls. "She had fantastic taste in everything, even music. She was never wrong on values; she knew the great from the not-so-great."

Chanel herself was one of the great ones. In the words of Maurice Sachs, bon vivant and chronicler of the era: "Her influence went beyond the reach of her work. Her name was etched on minds in the same way as the names of personages prominent in politics or letters. She represented, in sum, a new being. . . ."

ABOVE: *Splendid Venetian blackamoors at either side of the entrance doors for years welcomed the fortunate to Coco Chanel's private apartment within the House of Chanel, on the rue Cambon, in Paris. The great fashion designer, whose career spanned half a century, frequently referred to the nègres as "living personalities; they keep me company." Beyond the beckoning blackamoors is the small Foyer, a windowless rectangular room paneled in mirrors and antique Chinese screens. One of a collection of sculpted lions reigns from a glass-topped table set against a mirrored wall. Chanel once said: "I'm a bee. That's part of my sign: the lion, the sun. Women born under this sign are faithful, brave and very hard working . . . that's my character. I'm a bee born under the sign of the lion."*

An elaborate double-eagle mirror, mounted on mirror, serves as a clue to the opulence of the small third floor spaces where Coco Chanel spent most of her waking hours; she slept in another apartment, tiny, undistinguished, in the Ritz Hotel, across the street. Her sumptuous private world in the House of Chanel remains—an elegant shrine, a testament to a legendary arbiter of taste.

OPPOSITE: *The famous sweeping mirrored staircase leads from the Chanel salon on the first two floors to the couturiere's sumptuous apartment. Surrounded by a coterie of friends, Chanel would sit on the stairs to watch her mannequins show the collections, her strong but slight image intensified by the multiple reflections of many-faceted mirrors. Coco Chanel, "with a black sweater and ten rows of pearls, had revolutionized fashion," said Christian Dior. She also liberated women from corsets, made short hair and suntans fashionable; taught women to wear costume jewelry, slacks, culottes, shell-rimmed glasses, backless shoes and navy blue blazers; and to have real pockets in their clothes. And she gave her name to a suit that became a fashion classic.*

The Chanel touch, in interior design as well as fashion, was widely copied. "It is amazing how you find so many, many houses in Paris today that show her influence," says Paris publisher Hervé Mille.

Views of Coco Chanel's luxurious Living Room reveal her highly original character and confident taste. The complicated décor of the room includes eleven tables, two chairs and a sofa, objets d'art and twenty-two panels of Coromandel screens. OPPOSITE: *The screens create an alcove at one end of the room, framing a composition that includes a tapestry-covered Louis XV fauteuil, Chinese painting and altar table, and an*

assemblage of richly bound rare books. The adornments are Chinese: large deer and horses, porcelain bowls, and a serene Buddha. Jute-upholstered walls have been lacquered in gold. BELOW: *More bookshelves and screen panels provide the backdrop for an elaborately carved and gilded Régence table; sharing the marble top are a rock crystal lamp, a Chinese stele, and a Florentine gilt relief.*

69

A pair of bronze deer seem to graze near the Living Room
fireplace, which is surrounded by carvings from an Italian
church. In close quarters on the mantelpiece are a Sumerian
lion, a fourth-century B.C. Greek marble Aphrodite, a Coptic
head and a Bavarian bear. The bronze andirons were created
by Jacques Lipchitz, in the 1930s. A sheaf of wheat against the
wall is reiterated by the base of the glass-topped table, whose
form is in turn restated by a bouquet of crystal flowers Chanel
found at the Paris Flea Market. A rich Coromandel screen
punctuates the wall on the right.

"My nicest journeys take place on this couch," Chanel said of the famous suede-covered Living Room sofa where she napped—with her hat on—and from which she engaged friends in stimulating and often lengthy conversations. A stalk of wheat by Dali is the only painting in the apartment. Chanel didn't collect paintings. "Because I can't see. I don't want to walk around my house with glasses on my nose."

The lacquered table holds mementos of past loves: a golden box from the Duke of Westminster, and a small Picasso pencil drawing of poet Pierre Reverdy, slipped under the glass top.

ABOVE: *A table beside the Living Room sofa holds an abundance of precious objects: a pair of Chinese enameled deer, shell boxes, a Fabergé bear, carvings of camels, a Merovingian enameled cross. A gilt bronze by Caffiéri nestles among the rare books behind the sofa. Chanel loved gold; she used objects of quality in gold to give color; it was the color, not the value, that interested her. The Coromandel screens at both ends of the sofa wall camouflage doorways to other rooms.*

LEFT AND OPPOSITE: *Guests dined with Chanel in an atmosphere of subtle colors but extravagant surfaces and scale. The Louis XIII Dining Room table and suede-covered Louis XVI chairs rest on a Savonnerie rug. Along the textured fabric-covered walls are elaborate octagonal Spanish mirrors, Baroque consoles with voluptuously carved bases, a Louis XV mantel and mirror, and more Coromandel screens. The rock crystal chandelier is French. "She used mirrors to enlarge proportions and develop perspective," says Hervé Mille.*

"She never bought anything she didn't like," remarks M. Mille. "She didn't buy because it was valuable. She hated furniture for furniture, jewels for jewels, precious stones as stones. She was a connoisseur by intuition."

MARY TYLER MOORE

Mr. and Mrs. Grant Tinker (Mary Tyler Moore) called on John Hall to design their new house in Malibu because they had liked his interiors for the Allan Burnses' home. Mr. Burns co-created The Mary Tyler Moore Show.

Although Mr. Hall had more than the usual exposure to show business, since his parents were interior designers for many motion picture stars in the "Old Hollywood" days, he was personally, as well as professionally, curious. What is Mary Tyler Moore really like? The designer explains: "I had admired her for years, but knew only the television image. Sometimes you have to search for a key—something personal—that enables you to design an interior that truly reflects the client."

Mr. Hall was literally handed that key—eighteen squares of needlepoint. "Here. This is my house!" exclaimed the actress, at their first meeting.

John Hall, normally unflappable, recalls: "When she walked in with this stack, it was sort of frightening. My first thought was to blend them in, but when I learned Mary had been stitching away between takes for six years, making needlepoint for the day she and Grant would move into their first important home, I knew that was it. So we made the needlepoint central to the interior. Incidentally, the television crew put the number of Mary's stitches at one million."

The scope of the project went far beyond a million needlepoint stitches. The building and remodeling and interior décor took close to a year and a half. "By the time the house was completed, it was almost entirely new," Mr. Hall recalls. "Certainly it is the most complete interior design job I have ever done."

The house, in the Malibu Colony, a celebrity enclave, was Lana Turner's former residence. A subsequent owner had left it unoccupied for years, and it had fallen into serious disrepair. There were two lots, with the house in the middle. Part of the structure was cut away and half of the property was used as the site for another house. The remainder was sold to the Tinkers.

Operating on the theory that part of a house is better than none, the Tinkers built around a spiral staircase and part of the old living room. A section of a crumbling swimming pool was replaced by most of the new living room, while some of the pool area was decked and landscaped. A large glass-walled terrace came next. It faces, almost touches, the ocean. The present structure comprises 6,000 square feet, the only remaining features of the old house being the stairway and the entry.

The interior design began when the architectural plans were originally formulated, and Mr. Hall met weekly with the Tinkers or with Mrs. Tinker alone. "We really worked closely. She was so professional, so decisive. I would drive up to the house every Saturday and lay out the plans for the next week. If something wasn't right, I'd correct it that week and in the meantime work on other areas. We made every moment count."

For the interior Mr. Hall found ways to use everything especially meaningful to the Tinkers—furniture, art and objects they had kept throughout several moves made necessary by their television careers. Trophies and plaques are arranged on a wall in the billiard room, where Grant Tinker set up his snooker table. "Grant is from New England," Mr. Hall remarks. "He likes things low key and conservative, so we did his dressing room in stripes, very tailored. We used browns and beiges, and some green and white from the master bedroom."

The airy master suite, with its cheerful ambience and high ceilings, is like a separate apartment, with its own spectacular views of the Pacific. The main fabric is green and white—Mrs. Tinker's favorite combination, according to Mr. Hall. "She likes things bright, the brighter the better. The needlepoint is all colors of the rainbow, very springlike and gay. It really did set the mood for the interior very successfully." From the larger needlepoint pieces he made loose-back cushions for the custom-designed living room sofas.

It was difficult to envision a floor covering that would work well with the needlepoint. Then one day Mr. Hall and Mrs. Tinker happened to see carpet samples in a display window, arranged in a way that reminded them of Mondrian. "We realized that the idea was the solution to our rug problem," says Mr. Hall.

He and Mrs. Tinker sketched a pattern and specified custom-dyed colors to match the needlepoint.

The rug does indeed work with the sofas, its bold geometry serving as the major chords to counterpoint arpeggios of leaves and flowers.

John Hall completed the main conversation grouping in the living room with a contemporary table, which he designed and had made by the staff of craftsmen in his workshop. The workshop had been created years ago by his father to make fine reproductions of antique furniture when the right piece could not be found.

Although the French chairs upholstered in black-and-white fabric of herringbone design, which form another conversation group in the living room, and the oak-and-chestnut convent table in the dining room, are period pieces, antiques are relatively few in this interior design. The Tinkers wanted a special look and feeling to their home, sophisticated enough for formal entertaining and casual enough to be comfortable. The Malibu house is a house at the beach, but it is not a typical beach house. It is, rather, a townhouse by the sea.

LEFT: *Mr. and Mrs. Grant Tinker completely rebuilt Lana Turner's former Malibu Colony residence, creating an all-year-round beachfront house that is sunny and cheerful, a faithful, substantial reflection of the famous Mary Tyler Moore personality.*

BELOW: *Mrs. Tinker wanted her home designed around a collection of needlepoint squares, which she had been stitching on the set between takes for six years. So interior designer John Hall incorporated the gay floral needlework into the Living Room sofas and underscored it with a colorful custom patchwork carpet whose geometric style is suggestive of Mondrian. French doors open to a brick terrace and the Pacific Ocean beyond. The painting is by Robert Frame.*

The Tinkers wanted a comfortable, rather than an awesome, atmosphere in which to entertain their guests. The Dining Room has an informal country feeling, with reflected light from the ocean shining through a stained-glass window. A painted iron chandelier hangs above the 13-foot-long oak-and-chestnut convent refectory table. Candles in turned wooden holders reiterate the hue of painted Queen Anne-style chairs.

RIGHT: *A large arched window in the second floor Master Bathroom admits a captivating view of the surf. The light mood is amplified by a fresh green-on-white leaf pattern for walls and ceiling, combined with pleated bathtub drapery in a contrasting sunny color.*

BELOW: *The cheerful ambience is particularly evident in the large Master Suite—an upbeat refuge for the Tinkers returning late from the studio after exceptionally long working days. On the second floor, facing the ocean, it is almost a separate apartment. Here, with the sound of waves as accompaniment, Mrs. Tinker may spend leisure hours writing letters at the desk or relaxing on a sofa in front of the fireplace—doing more needlepoint. Green is a favorite color, used liberally for the carpeting and on walls, bed and upholstered pieces. Designer Hall specified pristine woodwork to lighten the visual weight of interior architectural beams.*

OPPOSITE: *The large brick Terrace is particularly suitable for beachfront living and entertaining. Outdoor furniture shares space with potted plants and trees, protected from ocean breezes by a wall of glass. The spiral stairway, part of the original Lana Turner house, leads to the master bedroom balcony.*

PABLO

"From the time I was seventeen years old, I was fascinated by cosmetics. My father was furious at first—'All those powderpuffs,' he scoffed."

Engaging and droll, Count Paolo Michelangelo Zappi-Manzoni, known to the fashion world as Pablo, goes on: "But I am living proof that if you are allowed by intelligent parents to do what you want, it can work out happily and successfully."

Women all over the world have turned to him for guidance. A pacesetter in his art, winner of the Coty American Fashion Critics Award, he substantially affects the way contemporary women look. Pablo is the creative director and makeup man *extraordinaire* for Elizabeth Arden, as well as international spokesman for the firm.

The youthful aristocrat was the only son among three children. His sisters also have distinguished themselves, one as a doctor, the other as a language professor at Milan University. The family is close, and Pablo returns annually to be with them, although they no longer gather in the vast family residence, in Italy. Used by the allies as a hospital during World War II, it was later sold.

Three months of the year Pablo seeks milder weather in such places as Positano, Corfu or Acapulco. The rest of the time he spends in his Park Avenue apartment, where he has concocted his own little Renaissance drama, guided by a friend, interior designer Count Raimondo "Dino" Corini.

"He helped me with the concept. I wanted a multicolored, multistyle effect—something to express me—an Italian," Pablo confides.

Without New York's insistent sounds, the apartment might well be in the palazzo of the Manzoni family in Bologna. The few family heirlooms Pablo chose to bring when he came to the United States, in 1964, reflect a taste for the spectacular: A pair of gilt cupids that once supported a cradle now form the base of a marble-topped console in the living room. A huge and rather overwhelming portrait, of the Tintoretto School, dominates a hallway. Italian laws concerning the preservation of national treasures prohibited the frame's being taken out of the country. "It had Vatican seals on it and was truly sublime," Pablo recalls tenderly. However, he has designed a very successful replacement for the original frame. Below the picture is a *cassapanca*, a small fourteenth-century chest, on which stands a bronze by Caroline Newhouse.

Because Pablo dislikes wallpaper and is bored by bland paint, the walls have been striated in a soft coffee color on white, lacquered in paint enriched with gallons of clear nail polish. This bit of ingenuity, and the inspirational addition of green *faux-marbre* moldings,

emphatically place the apartment in the European genre. There is also a thoroughly continental flair in the way Pablo marches paintings, plaques and mirrors up the walls to utilize height and space.

There is nothing in the least disjointed about the amusing mix of furniture styles. After all, any palace of consequence has treasures accumulated from many periods. In Pablo's apartment, a Queen Anne secretary joins company with Venetian chairs and French banquettes. Two Spanish sofas companion a William and Mary sideboard and an Irish table, in the living room.

Everywhere there are candles—the sign of a romantic spirit. Everywhere too are frog figures—a large white frog filled with dried flowers; stone frogs; bronze frogs. "They are ugly, frogs, but terribly dignified," Pablo observes. "They stare with those big eyes, like a Buddha. I love them. They are regal, so enigmatic."

A Fu dog lurks behind one of the draperies in the living room. The Irish table holds bronze doré figures—including an elephant, a crocodile and a rhinoceros—made by his friend the Italian artist Count Monte Ceconi.

There is no dining room, yet Pablo loves to entertain, so he has placed easily movable chairs and stools near the two Spanish sofas and against the walls. The room is open and fluid enough to accommodate a sizable group gracefully. "I don't believe in having guests serve themselves from the buffet. All those people jammed together—horrible! I have my guests served."

However, because plates must be balanced on laps, this enthusiastic cook says, "You wouldn't believe what I have devised for dinner without a knife. After all, you can't have beef à la Bourguignonne every night."

Dark brown moiré, mellowed by sunlight, covers the Spanish sofas and is repeated in the bedroom headboard, spread and draperies. The effect is soft and quiet. Somberness is alleviated by a sprinkling of tapestry, gold brocade on stools, and the vibrant hues of scattered Chinese porcelain jars.

A French six-panel leather screen painted with allegorical figures was discovered at an auction; separated, the panels are used as wall hangings. Not only are they beautiful, but as strong verticals they emphasize the graceful height of the ceilings.

"It makes the room, don't you think? So much better than lots of little things all over," Pablo observes, making a grimace of disapproval at such a notion.

Leaning against a door frame as he surveys his living room, he emanates the grace and serenity of old-world noblesse, and these very personal rooms are endowed with the same spirit of charm and mystery so characteristic of this master of illusion.

Internationally famed makeup artist Count Paolo Michelangelo Zappi-Manzoni created a radiant Renaissance countenance for his small Park Avenue apartment. He discovered at auction a French six-panel allegorical cuir peint screen, which, framed as individual figure panels, adorns the Living Room.
OPPOSITE: When Elizabeth Arden introduced the young Italian aristocrat to the United States, in 1964, he brought with him a few choice heirlooms from his family's vast palazzo in Bologna, including an extravagant pair of cupids that once supported a sixteenth-century Florentine cradle.
BELOW: A menagerie in bronze doré, sculpted by Count Monte Ceconi, on an Irish drop-leaf table, gilds the European mélange.

Another view of the Living Room reveals a Queen Anne
chinoiserie-lacquered secretary attended by a French tapestry-
and-giltwood tabouret. Nearby, an upholstered screen backdrops
a needlepoint Louis XIII armchair and two antique tables.
Above the secretary a French double-sunburst clock spreads its
rays against the soft-toned wall. Pablo striated the walls
throughout the apartment in a coffee color over white, then
lacquered them in paint enriched—fittingly—with gallons of
clear nail polish.

For a man with no dining room, Pablo entertains with aplomb.
He transformed half of the Kitchen into an area well suited to
sophisticated dining à deux. A French cuir peint screen and
storage doors with murals by the Florentine artist Alfio
Rapisardi create an intimate environment for an
eighteenth-century Irish mahogany breakfast table and Genovese
chairs. When he entertains large groups, guests balance plates
on their laps, in the adjoining living room; Pablo deplores the
usual buffet crush, so dinner is served to each guest.

Views of the Bedroom continue the sophisticated old-world atmosphere.

ABOVE: Sunlight has mellowed a deep-toned
moiré used for the headboard, bedspread and
drapery. A walnut settee and chair and a
burl secretary are seventeenth-century pieces.
A photograph of opera diva Maria Callas
rests on the French Provincial desk. Flanking
an Italian Renaissance battle scene above the
headboard are "two ugly big-nosed Roman
emperors" on marble portrait plaques. Says
Pablo: "It is my terror that they will fall
down one night and break the mirrored night
tables all to bits."

LEFT: A friendly lion sculpture reigns from
atop a seventeenth-century armoire from
Umbria, while a Louis XIII chair covered in
figural needlepoint attends the desk.

Vignettes of the Bedroom offer personalized insights.
ABOVE: *A silver tankard with lid, on Pablo's work desk, holds writing and drawing implements. "Miss Arden gave it to me," he remarks. Close by are a pillbox from Persia and a string of worry beads brought from Greece, both in turquoise.*

LEFT: *Octagonal bedside tables are a trompe l'oeil achievement by Piero Yengo, who marbleized the completely mirrored surfaces to resemble three-color inlay. Cornice moldings in bedroom and living room are also marbleized, an effect that intrigues the noted master of illusion. His distinguished work in the fashion world and the continental style of his residence both exhibit Pablo's sure, deft touch.*

SENATOR EDWARD M. KENNEDY

Rich gleaming woods of distinguished American and English antiques; a cove ceiling, created especially for a treasured seventeenth-century Dutch brass chandelier; waterfowl decoys from a notable collection—all reveal the personal tastes of Senator and Mrs. Edward M. Kennedy in their first permanent residence.

The two-level house in McLean, Virginia, on a seven-acre site overlooking the Potomac River, was completed in 1968 by San Francisco architect John Carl Warnecke and New York interior designers Keith Irvine and Thomas Fleming, who met the Kennedys through another client, Mrs. Aristotle Onassis.

"The Kennedys wanted an enormous living room opening to the outside," Mr. Irvine explains, "yet they preferred a basically traditional house. The solution was to give the effect of a modernized barn. Then we had an architectural background to play off against."

The result is an expansive upstairs drawing room, with beams that soar to thirty-two feet. "The space is much less pretentious than it might have been," Mr. Fleming comments, "even with that enormous volume." The room has three main seating arrangements, as well as a favorite activity area around the grand piano.

With a number of bold strokes, the designers gave confident accents to the vast space that had to be controlled. "We were keen to have a mantel of exceptional quality," Mr. Irvine explains. "Then the rug was next. We chose a large Oushak because it mixes beautifully and warmly with traditional furniture."

"The next problem," Mr. Fleming continues, "was what to do with all those windows. Whatever we used for curtains had to be very simple—but very strong." Mrs. Kennedy agreed on a brilliant taffeta, exactly the vibrant note they were seeking.

Because there was strength in the warm woods and pure shapes of the Kennedys' antiques, the designers urged a bit of lightheartedness in the purchase of two important Chinese Chippendale chairs, widely copied since they first appeared, about 1780. "Fantasy chairs, you know," says Mr. Irvine, smiling. "They're very comfortable and in beautiful condition." This buoyant feeling is sustained by a fresh young chintz, counterpointed by yellow and white damasks and constantly changing outdoor greenery.

The same easy youthful spirit pervades the remainder of the house. When the senator told Mr. Fleming that his favorite color was mauve, they used the color with considerable dash in the library, with a masculine plaid, accented by several pieces of heirloom pewter, which Mrs. Kennedy brought from their Hyannis Port house.

Although Mr. Kennedy has his own small study, the library is where the family loves to gather. "He was very keen to have barn siding and stone," the designers relate, "and the only way we could achieve that beautiful weathered effect was actually to buy some old barns. That's how we got the paneling and those beams."

Another of the senator's special touches is the large collection of antique decoys, which can be seen nesting comfortably in the library, living room and hallways throughout the house.

The dining room is distinctly traditional. Because a back injury, sustained in a plane crash, still troubles the senator, he was determined to avoid the fragile whimsies of antique dining chairs. Ten good Newport reproductions were the secure alternative. The square table was also the senator's idea. It is a specially constructed replica of a Hepplewhite table belonging to the Duke of Devonshire. The square shape is a particular preference of Senator Kennedy's because he feels that the very nature of such a seating plan—two to a side—draws a group closer together and stimulates the conversational flow.

Perhaps the most striking note in the dining room is an exquisite screen covered in wallpaper depicting Boston Harbor in the nineteenth century. The paper is an original from the famous "Scenic America" series by Zuber, a complete set of which now adorns the walls of a White House reception room. Other White House memories are evoked by graceful silver service plates once used by President and Mrs. John F. Kennedy.

If there is one room in the house that is "pure Joan Kennedy," it is the master bedroom. White and pink and green, it perfectly complements her fair coloring.

"She was immediately drawn to the fabric," Mr. Irvine explains, indicating the hand-printed canvas that pervades the room on draperies, bed and canopy. Sunlight pours over puffy upholstered pieces, a pine mantelpiece and desk, and white silk walls.

Mr. Irvine is pleased with a room that so happily accords with his own philosophy. "I have a strong feeling that bedrooms should be very feminine," he comments. "Men, we find, enjoy the sense of ease and luxury generated by fabrics and design too often considered appropriate only for their wives. In the bedroom a man should have a sense of belonging, of being enveloped by the surroundings that please his wife."

"Mrs. Kennedy is marvelous to work with," designers Irvine and Fleming observe enthusiastically. "She is very open to suggestion, very eager to know about everything. She doesn't dictate; she probes and learns."

Intelligence is a continuous presence here—poise without affectation, a family trait realized in a distinguished American home.

Senator and Mrs. Edward Kennedy decided on a traditional style for their permanent residence, in Virginia, and they needed a comfortable, practical home for their active and growing family.

BELOW: *The Entrance Hall ceiling was specially designed to accommodate a seventeenth-century Dutch brass chandelier hanging above an English rent table. In the alcove stands a diminutive Rhode Island broken-pediment chest-on-chest. A few of Senator Kennedy's antique decoys rest in front of a seventeenth-century Massachusetts corner cupboard, on the right.*

OPPOSITE: *The Living Room displays a pearwood Chippendale mantelpiece, never painted, which was brought from a manor house in England. Chinese Export tureens and Blue John urns decorate the mantel. The eighteenth-century English desk was used by the late Ambassador Joseph P. Kennedy in London.*

FOLLOWING PAGES: *A window wall in the Living Room emphasizes the luxuriant view that changes with the seasons. Designers Keith Irvine and Thomas Fleming decided on a modernized barn effect, with a high ceiling and exposed beams to keep the room airy and unpretentious. The shield-back chair in the foreground is English Hepplewhite. An early-nineteenth-century Oushak rug, large enough to unify the floor area, mixes warmly with the traditional furniture. The cane-seated high chair is eighteenth-century American.*

RIGHT AND BELOW: *A close look at two seating areas in the Living Room shows more distinguished antiques. One of a pair of Chippendale bamboo chairs with original paint is a particularly important piece. The table lamp under the mirror is nineteenth-century French porcelain.*

OPPOSITE: *An unusual eighteenth-century American walnut secretary stands in another corner of the Living Room. One of a pair of carved and gilded Chippendale mirrors hangs above an American Pembroke table displaying family pictures. Martha Washington and Queen Anne chairs are period pieces, although reproductions are used often in the house for the sake of sturdiness. The carved head from a sarcophagus was given to the Kennedys when they visited Egypt.*

OPPOSITE: *Silver plates, a gift from Mrs. Joseph P. Kennedy, and an old Irish silver service highlight the traditional Dining Room. The Kennedys chose the square Hepplewhite table design because the two-to-a-side seating works well for spirited conversation. Wallpaper on the screen, depicting Boston Harbor in the nineteenth century, is from a famous series by the Swiss artist Zuber, called "Scenic America," a complete set of which appears in a White House reception room.*

LEFT: *The Library is paneled with weathered wood taken from old barns sought for the purpose. Two sofas in a deeply shaded plaid linen make up the main conversation grouping in front of a warming fire. The Seal of the Commonwealth of Massachusetts hangs on the stone chimneypiece near an American lowboy.*

BELOW: *The Master Bedroom design incorporates soft colors that flatter Mrs. Kennedy's fair complexion. Senator Kennedy painted the picture above the bed while in the hospital recovering from a plane crash.*

SYBIL CONNOLLY

Sybil Connolly, the brilliant Irish fashion designer, thinks she might have become a designer of interiors. "The way one looks and the way one lives are usually connected," she says. "I think the colors one likes to wear and see worn are also the colors one likes to live with."

A second career may not be imminent for Miss Connolly, but it is certainly indicated. A similar aesthetic informs her philosophy of fashion and interior design. Harmony is the key—in color, in scene, in mood. She shuns shock tactics. "Use nothing that startles; beauty is the only stimulation needed."

Above all, Miss Connolly dislikes pretension. In fashion, her designs are understated. In houses, "museum rooms" and "shop windows" are anathema. "When you come into a room, you want to have an overall feeling of something attractive and beautiful that makes you feel easy," she observes. "Perfection is not human and we shouldn't pretend that it is. The ideal house should look lived in, as if somebody reads the books on the shelves."

Given the designer's predilection for classicism, comfort and good design, it is not surprising that she is enthusiastic about "our Dublin squares" and their classic eighteenth-century townhouses, or that she expresses a preference for the great English country houses. "In the connection between the English house and garden there is a softness and kinship one doesn't feel in the French châteaux, which, although beautiful, are captured by a more formal architectural plan."

Miss Connolly's main residence, which houses the famous boutique with its Adam-style moldings and plasterwork, is a classic eighteenth-century building. The architecture dictates period design and furnishings.

Her mews house, at the end of the garden, is a special favorite, decorated with prized family pieces and custom-printed linen to harmonize with the classic setting.

"When it came to doing the house, I thought to myself, perhaps I should do it with indigenous things. My clothes had been a success because they were indigenous. All designers—Italian, Spanish, French, English— draw from their native countries. I wanted to dig deep into what we have in Ireland," she explains.

Linen was one answer—the finest of handkerchief linen, woven in Ireland, and pleated. The material is so fine that nine yards pleat into one yard. It took a thousand yards to cover the walls of the high-ceilinged rooms of the boutique. It's been on the walls now for over fifteen years—pale gray, with an unexpected touch of lavender. The unusual covering has been a sensation.

The two upper floors are Miss Connolly's private domain. "Here I couldn't use only Irish fabrics," she comments, referring to the combination silk and wool chair covers, "but I used as many as I could."

Every visitor falls in love with the dining room, perhaps because of the fuchsia wallpaper. The designer chose it because fuchsias grow wild in Ireland.

"The table comes from a house in County Limerick," she relates. "The people who owned it are direct descendants of one of the knights who killed Thomas à Becket." She slips from the historical aside to a design decision made with a certain amount of trepidation. The mahogany antique was "ebonized" to match the ebony-and-gilt dining chairs, made in 1820. "It could have been a disaster but it worked out all right."

She tracks down what she wants with verve and efficiency. One instance is the stairway in her mews house. Years ago, author and historian Desmond Guinness told her about a house outside Kilkenny, a small early-eighteenth-century house with a Chinese Chippendale staircase. When she was in the area she went to see it. "All the rooms were rounded and there was this staircase that I had been longing to see—it was a sort of country Chinese Chippendale, and oh, so beautiful. The owner allowed me to photograph it and I had it copied for my little house," Miss Connolly explains.

And in the mews house her fabled eye for unusual effect within the classic mold is everywhere evident. The bedroom is a good example. Miss Connolly had inherited some lovely late-eighteenth-century porcelain of the Angoulême design, issued in honor of the marriage of Marie Antoinette's daughter to the Duke of Angoulême. "I discovered that a shop in London made a wallpaper in this design, and then I coaxed the Irish textile industry to print it on linen. The bed and the windows are all draped with this Angoulême fabric."

The dining room of the little house is blue and white, a color theme that is an obvious favorite, extended with a flair in her collection of Irish delftware.

"It's fun, collecting something that is almost impossible to find," she confides of her fascination for the ware. "I started over fifteen years ago. A Captain Delamain made this type of porcelain in the mid-eighteenth century, for only eighteen years."

In all ways the legendary designer is a collector of the unusual and beautiful. She calls her collection "a conglomerate," but the unifying thread is harmony. "The best of each century *should* go together, really."

Whether Egyptian antiques or a Sicilian bowl circa A.D. 700 or a bouquet of French chatelaines pinned on a cushion, the exquisite workmanship charms her and confirms her credo: "Beauty stimulates. Beauty gives pleasure to the eye and rings the soul with harmony. When beauty is there, it doesn't have to be explained."

The Main House

Old bricks and a delicate fanlight frame the original eighteenth-century entrance to the fashionable world of Irish couturiere Sybil Connolly. Purchased in 1957, the Georgian building on Merrion Square in Dublin is Miss Connolly's main residence; two lower floors are devoted to a boutique and showroom, while two upper floors comprise her private domain. There is also a small mews house, at the end of a charming garden.

"Our Dublin squares are some of the only eighteenth-century ones left in Europe," says Miss Connolly. "So I hope they'll always be preserved. The red brick façades are so pretty, and after two hundred years they have a sort of a pink color. They're absolutely classic eighteenth-century townhouses."

The gentle warmth that pervades the main-house is underscored by the Living Room's subtle tones. Collectables such as the arrangement against the fireplace wall of Chinese Export plates, circa 1735, add color highlights as well as visual interest. The wall brackets are Chinese Chippendale; the French cartel is eighteenth century. A Chinese vase containing buoyant Matilija poppies rests on an eighteenth-century Chinese lacquered chest, which serves as a table.

"I don't think there is anything that startles, in my house," Miss Connolly says. "It is a sort of blending of different periods and moods, because I like harmony in philosophy, music, painting—in everything. I don't like chaos or shock tactics." The designer adds: "The eighteenth-century feeling is the mood I happen to enjoy most. That century was such a prolific period for good design."

LEFT: *Light enters the Living Room through large delicately mullioned windows draped in floral-print Irish fabric; a coordinating geometric pattern covers a Louis XVI fauteuil. The round table holds a collection of tiny boxes, while beyond the poppies a Venetian mirror hangs above a chinoiserie lacquered chest, circa 1690.*

BELOW LEFT: *"My Dining Room is a room that everyone loves," says Miss Connolly, "and everything is Irish." The fuchsia wallpaper is a tribute to the flower that grows wild in Ireland. Ebony and gilt Regency dining chairs, circa 1820, surround an antique mahogany table "ebonized" to match. Waterford crystal, circa 1800, delicate lace place mats and Georgian silver confirm the room's Irish heritage. Miss Connolly inherited the circa 1785 French porcelain—and also had the motif duplicated in fabric for her bedroom.*

BELOW: *A brightly lined niche in the Library displays to advantage a collection of shells from California and some of the rare Dublin delftware the designer has sought out.*

A motif based upon Miss Connolly's heirloom French porcelain pattern known as **Angoulême** characterizes her Bedroom; she urged the Irish textile industry to print it, from an existing wallpaper design she found in London, on the linen fabric used throughout the room. The pattern was originally issued in honor of the marriage of Marie Antoinette's daughter to the Duke of Angoulême. A seventeenth-century French ivory crucifix hangs against the lavishly gathered baldachin fabric. A pot of garden flowers adds a bright spot of contrasting color to the monochromatic scheme.

"I'm rather shy about saying that my favorite color is green," admits Miss Connolly. "I love green and white—my bedroom is basically green and white. I also love blue and white; but I think you've got to have another color with it—a touch of bandbox red or green, because just all blue and white is quite dull and cold." The crocheted afghan seems to symbolize the handcrafts industries that have been revitalized as a result of the great acceptance of Sybil Connolly's clothes.

The amply draped dressing table in Miss Connolly's Bedroom, standing between tall French doors, makes a distinctive statement of graceful flowing line and unerring proportion. Regency pelmets, extravagantly wrapped and draped with fabric, frame the doors and emphasize the room's generous ceiling height. A well-shaped Louis XV tabouret refines and restates the central form of the composition. The lacquered mirror adds another element of precise geometry.

"I think my bedroom gets the most comment," says Miss Connolly. "The Angoulême linen has been a great success, I must say that. In fact, Nancy Lancaster, who has been in my house in Dublin and who everybody says has the best taste in the world, once wrote me and asked, 'May I copy your bedroom?' So we printed all the linen I had for her. Then, two years later, she wrote and said that one of the very rich South African families had seen the Angoulême linen in her bedroom and wanted to know if I could get more linen printed. It rather amused me that this was going so far around."

The Mews House

A winding brick walk leads from the main house, past a prosperous rose bed edged by a curve of lavender, to the small mews house. Aged stone walls, grown over with vines and tree foliage, help establish privacy and a countrified feeling for the carefully tended garden. Says Miss Connolly: "I've replanted it all, with help from Russell Page's sister, who lives in Ireland. You've got to be very patient with gardens, you know. Of course, it's a town garden—not very big, but sort of fun."

The charming mews house also is eighteenth-century, with classic period architectural details and a sunny hospitable atmosphere. The two glass-paneled center doors open directly into a long living room that runs along the width of the brick structure. Miss Connolly rebuilt her cozy "little house" with the assistance of two craftsmen, Michael Lally and Michael Hart. "I didn't even have an architect," she recalls, "which I think was rather courageous of me."

A clear view of the garden and the main house can be glimpsed from the central Hallway through the living room's glass-paneled doors. The pristine traditional molding and dado counterpoint a rich warm wall paint and matching chair cushion.

A mirror reflects part of the staircase that Miss Connolly copied from one in a small early-eighteenth-century house outside Kilkenny. She had first heard about it from Desmond Guinness. Years later when she was in the area she visited the house: "All the rooms were rounded and there was this staircase that I had been longing to see," she remembers. "It was sort of country Chinese Chippendale, and oh, so beautiful. The owners allowed me to photograph it and I had it copied for my little house." Adds Miss Connolly: "I was terribly ambitious, to take on such a project."

Bright blooms fill the lemon-fresh Living Room—on chintz, in vases, on porcelain. The design is open and airy, with lightly scaled antique tables counterpointing comfortable furniture. The floor is marbleized in three shades of the same color, adding perspective. Niches at either side of a George I mirror contain a collection of nineteenth-century English china.

Plaster shells enrich the cornicework. "In the eighteenth century they often used plaster shells as decorative objects," Miss Connolly explains. "The American designer Tony Duquette took me to a place in California where I bought wonderful shells, some of which I've had duplicated on the cornice." Walls the color of sunshine complement the vibrant, yet still soft, scheme. "In the eighteenth century, and much earlier, interiors were very colorful," says the designer. "Not harsh colors or startling colors—they were fresh and cheerful and easy to live with."

A bookcase wall in the Living Room offers display space for a variety of treasured objects. A deep-set niche holds nineteenth-century English china. Reading material rests casually atop a sturdy 1810 writing table.

"I think a house has to look as if people live there," says Miss Connolly. "To have it too perfect, and the objects too much in place, is wrong. I won't say that it should be untidy, but it should look like somebody reads the books on the shelves and perhaps has taken one down and left it on the table. I rather like that. I think it's sort of friendly."

Fragile eighteenth-century Irish crystal girandoles stand at either end of a narrow console. Above is a sixteenth-century Ming painting on silk. The designer's taste in art is also distinctly traditional: "I think some modern art is interesting, but beauty shouldn't have to be explained."

A collection of Nanking plates provides the color scheme and main decoration for the simplified Dining Room. A centerpiece of fresh garden flowers adds the touch of another color Miss Connolly feels is so necessary to a blue-and-white scheme. Eighteenth-century French cane and painted wood chairs surround a sparingly set table. "I do love Irish silver, so I like to set the dining room table with Irish silver and Irish glassware," she says.

An eighteenth-century Rouen wall fountain is another addition to Miss Connolly's extensive porcelain collection. She is most intrigued by her assemblage of Irish delftware, which was made for only eighteen years, during the mid-eighteenth century, by a Captain Delamain, and had never been exhibited before 1971. Since the clay used for Liverpool and Bristol delftware was the same, and there were other similarities, recognizing Irish delftware requires expertise. "Even the curators at the Victoria and Albert, in London, say it's very difficult to be 100 percent sure," Miss Connolly explains, adding proudly, "but I think I can now say what is a piece of Irish."

Hydrangea-patterned chintz sets the frankly feminine tone of a light-filled Guest Bedroom. Two paint colors minimize the extreme ceiling height of this second floor room, while a fireplace promises snug warmth. A focal point is an elaborate lacquered dressing table, circa 1790. Other furnishings include a period French bench and a table set with memorabilia.

Miss Connolly's attitude toward room design coincides with her fashion philosophy: "A woman shouldn't be startling; when she passes by, one should feel, 'Goodness, how attractive!' A woman coming into a restaurant with an outrageous hat is not my idea of well dressed. And I think I feel the same way about the room I have done. When you come into a room you want to have an overall feeling of something attractive and beautiful that makes you feel easy, rather than to come in and say, straight away, 'Oh, goodness, look at that.' Nothing should stimulate more than beauty," she declares firmly. "What I try to achieve is a stimulating beauty." Certainly Sybil Connolly's living spaces represent Irish design, past and present, at its loveliest.

GAYELORD HAUSER

Gayelord Hauser has always been a source of fascination to his devoted followers. The London *Sunday Times* has named him "one of the makers of the twentieth century." "People treat me with reverence," he says with a smile. "I've been around such a long time."

There are those who imagine that the man who first advocated the healthful delights of yogurt, wheat germ, brewer's yeast and blackstrap molasses lives in a Spartan environment, where exercise boards, barbells and blenders are the chief items of décor, and where window boxes are planted with carrots and cucumbers.

Dr. Hauser does eat sparingly and exercise religiously, but he lives with the elegance that might be expected of a close friend of the late Lady Mendl, America's first major interior designer. His summer home, in Sicily, is a rather ornate house surrounded by acres of flowers. His winter residence, in California, is a French-style farmhouse with a courtyard, a simple cheerful house that can be managed with a small staff. The living room is his workroom, with light flooding in from the patio and garden.

Aesthetic guidance for the bright fresh look of the interiors came from Lady Mendl. "She said, 'Bring the garden into your home,'" Dr. Hauser recalls, "so I brought trees inside. Lady Mendl loved green and white and so do I. So many things are lost in this world of plastics. I'd rather have just one real flower than a whole basket of artificial ones."

The late Frey Brown, Dr. Hauser's longtime business associate, and designer Miriam Whelan worked together to give the Beverly Hills residence "a European look compatible with the California style of living." For the most part they used pieces already owned by Dr. Hauser.

"I bought many things in my travels, and everything here has a history, but Mr. Brown did the assembling. He had the taste," Dr. Hauser says emphatically. "He knew just how to arrange everything."

Dr. Hauser has some outstanding paintings, mostly French, a variety of unusual objets d'art—a favorite being a miniature replica of the column in the Place Vendôme, carved with scenes depicting events in French history—and perhaps the most valuable collection of porcelain and faïence fruits and vegetables in the world.

"Everything that I have is something that pleased me and still does," Dr. Hauser comments. He points out a sunny Saint-Severin, a Renoir, a Picasso and a Buffet. Most of the paintings were collected long ago. "Luckily I chose things that are very precious now," he remarks, "but I bought them to fit at the time. They still do."

The collection of fruits and vegetables is justly famous. Many of the finest specimens were gifts from Lady Mendl and the Duchess of Windsor.

The Hauser repertoire of anecdotes, related in a variety of accents—for the nutritionist is a famed mimic—is as fabled as his collection of recipes. Schweitzer, Ghandi, Perón, the Windsors—their paths crossed his, time and time again—and Gayelord Hauser loves to recount details with his almost total recall.

A recent dinner guest whose great interest is chandeliers was asked what she thought of the Empire crystal chandelier hanging above Dr. Hauser's dining room table. She admitted she hadn't even noticed it, because she had been so fascinated by her host. "I can't even remember the menu," she said, without a trace of embarrassment. "He was telling such wonderful stories about the Duchess of Windsor, I don't think I glanced at the ceiling even once."

Dr. Hauser's conversation often turns to Hollywood and the great stars who came to him with problems and became his friends. Greta Garbo called one day, asking if she could come for a consultation; she was always tired. Thinking a friend was playing a practical joke, Dr. Hauser told the butler to ask her to come the following day when he wasn't so busy. She arrived, stayed for lunch—mostly yogurt—and became a close friend. The actress is a frequent house guest, so frequent, in fact, that Dr. Hauser's simply furnished guest house is her special retreat when she comes to California.

Gayelord Hauser likes to recall his eighty-first birthday party, given for him by Miss Garbo at his hilltop home. The actress, known for her reticence about mixing with large groups of people, took great joy in running the event, cooking with the nutritionist and even directing traffic for guests. "Because it was a special occasion," a friend remembers, "Dr. Hauser let us have a rich dessert and even served coffee."

Fundamentally people- and project-oriented, Gayelord Hauser is not so much concerned with décor as he is with his work. "I have a purpose," he states firmly. "When I first began as a professional, in Chicago in 1922, I said the happiness and health of the world depend on a new system of health science. Once I heard three senators on a television program talking about the atrocious food Americans eat. In summing up, one of them observed, 'We have gone to the moon, but we still have to walk blocks for a good loaf of bread.'"

In his eighties, he is stalwart proof of the efficacy of his theories. Lecturing here and abroad, writing—*Forbes* magazine once credited him with being the author of more books printed in more languages than any other man—traveling to Sicily for the summer, back to his Beverly Hills home in the winter, he seems to radiate health and enthusiasm for good living.

OPPOSITE: *Visitors to nutritionist/author Gayelord Hauser's Beverly Hills residence take immediate notice of the faïence vegetables, part of a unique collection, clustered atop an antique Florentine painted and gilded bombé chest in the Entrance Hall. Dr. Hauser found the elaborate Baroque mirror in Sicily, where he has a summer home. The potted blooms lining the walk reflect his love for gardening.*

LEFT: *The interiors display Dr. Hauser's paintings, porcelains and furnishings in a European setting compatible with California living. An arrangement of paintings in the Living Room includes works by Heckel, Picasso, Forain, Kirchner, Siniki, Khmeluk and Avery. The round glass-topped table with **faux-bamboo** legs was purchased at the Paris Flea Market.*

BELOW: *Another Living Room view reveals works by Asselin, Buffet, Creixams and Dufy. Next to the Italian Louis XV armchair by the fireplace is a miniature of the column in the Place Vendôme and a blackamoor-base table. In the niche and on the mantel are more of the nutritionist's porcelain vegetables.*

A cornucopia of fruits and vegetables, both real and faïence, garnishes the Dining Room. An Empire crystal chandelier above the antique Italian Provincial table adds a note of formality. Trompe l'oeil plates and serving dishes are arranged on a wall above the spread wings of a Georgian swan console; fruits and vegetables rest on its marble top. Many of the porcelain and faïence pieces were given to Dr. Hauser by the Duchess of Windsor, and by Lady Mendl, who also guided him in setting the garden-fresh tone of the interiors. Dr. Hauser plans to donate the extensive collection to a museum, eventually, "to pass on thirty or forty years of personal taste."

Many of Dr. Hauser's guests are celebrities who originally consulted him professionally and then became personal friends. Dinner table conversation is always stimulating; his stock of amusing anecdotes is as fabled as his ceramic collection, but the topic uppermost in the host's mind is a serious one—a new system of health science for the world.

111

PAULINE TRIGÈRE

The New York State countryside is dotted with old farmhouses taken in hand by a coterie of backwoods aficionados with a fondness for chintz and old pewter. Though there are many, few achieve that subtle blend of *haut chic* and suitability that guarantees success. But this Westchester County country house, the work of a fashion designer, is outstanding not only because of its individuality and charm, but because the interior projects the owner's talent and personal magnetism.

Pauline Trigère, French born but for years very much an American fashion influence, has been referred to as "the Chanel of America." She does not approve the designation, however. Although she agrees that Chanel used fabrics brilliantly, the designer herself prefers another comparison. "I think I am more like Vionnet. Yes, much more like Vionnet."

Pauline Trigère does accept one comparison with the legendary Chanel—her way with fabric. "Fabric is the dictator" is a Trigère pronouncement, and the designer practices it in her home as well as in her fashions.

"I guess there are several hundred yards of fabrics in the house," she estimates, being careful not to overstate the number; lack of precision would be very unlike Miss Trigère. Her signature, literally, is everywhere in the small-beamed guest bedroom, lush with Trigère-designed fabric from her fashion collection. The master bedroom fabric is a handsome red-and-white Matisse-inspired pattern. Still another bedroom is abloom with floral chintz—an old French pattern—a superbly appropriate background for the bed, which Miss Trigère had made from an old French *bonnetière,* a chest used in the 1800s for bonnets and hats. "I cut the *bonnetière* in half and put a bed in between," she explains.

When Pauline Trigère bought her 140-year-old farmhouse, nearly three decades ago, she immediately involved herself in a new and exciting design challenge. "The little farmhouse was nothing," she says, "but the land had large rocks, old apple trees and a pond. I was charmed." First came major additions—a new garden room, kitchen, dining room and second floor—then decorative touches. "Everything has been redone several times. At first I had no money; then I had no knowledge. I used to move a wall like I would move a buckle on a dress. It was expensive, but I have learned a great deal.

"I am a terribly critical person where my own work is concerned. I make mistakes sometimes," she concedes, "despite my experience—I've been designing fashions since 1937. Still, sometimes things just don't work out. The trick is to catch the mistake before it goes in the collection, and discard it before the show. Occasionally just the look on my model's face tells me something is wrong. Other times, I look at something in a new way, see it's wrong, remove it from the line or change it. I do the same thing with the house. Some things have not worked; I've done them over."

In Pauline Trigère's country home not all the pieces are European. With a designer's instinct for being in the right place at the right time, she just happened to discover at auction some superb tables from the old Fulton Café in Brooklyn.

"I bought four of the single black tables, had them cleaned, and found they were inlaid with gray and pink marble. Beautiful! So, I never put my doilies out."

The four original tables have become Miss Trigère's dining room table; the teakwood aprons have been removed to another part of the house. "I had benches and tables made from them, for the garden room. They're covered in a fabric that looks like silk but has to be vinyl, because we have so many dogs around here." A later purchase of four additional tables from the café provided material for a banister in the guest house.

In Paris Miss Trigère found a fireplace in a soft color like pewter, and decided it would work well in her dressing room. "In my bedroom," she explains, "I get enough heat from the back of the living room fireplace. But I do a lot of work in my dressing room; it needed the warmth and charm." The magnificent sixteenth-century chest and the old convent doors in the dining room were found in Spain by sheer luck at an auction.

"When I bought this place," she reminisces, "I had just designed the most beautiful gold turtle. Then I noticed how many live turtles were crawling about here. To name the house *La Tortue* was inevitable. Originally there were only a few turtles on the grounds. They're slow but they do have a way of multiplying."

The turtle theme proliferates inside the house as well. Pillows on a multiplicity of chairs are covered in the famous Trigère turtle print, in cotton and silk, and the designer often wears a robe of matching fabric.

A collection of well over six hundred turtles, fashioned variously of gold, silver, pewter, crystal and granite, comprises a charming diversity of sizes and uses: In addition to the purely ornamental, utilitarian pieces such as plates, ice cream molds, graters, even an antique hand warmer, all have the turtle motif.

For Pauline Trigère, weekends at her country house are a refuge from her hectic New York pace.

"If I'm tense or disturbed about anything I come here and work, sometimes out in the garden. I don't know whether or not the years of work I've put into it show as much as my time and effort on the interior, but the work and the love and imagination are there, all the same."

LEFT: *Fashion designer Pauline Trigère's rural New York State home is a 140-year-old Westchester County farmhouse; she purchased* La Tortue *more than 25 years ago.*

BELOW: *The Garden Room and adjoining dining room, part of a major addition, have a spacious indoor/outdoor atmosphere; the landscape, seen through large glass doors, is pleasingly pastoral and rocky. Mother-of-pearl inlaid teak benches and tables were made from the aprons of Chinese tables that once stood in Brooklyn's old Fulton Café; the upholstery resembles silk but is actually vinyl, in deference to the canine residents.*

OPPOSITE: *In the Living Room, turtle ornaments cover an old bowling game table with a thick oversize glass top that repeats the curve of the comfortable 12-foot floral-patterned sofa.*

OPPOSITE: *An intriguing collection of old and new faïence surrounds a sixteenth-century Spanish chest in the Dining Room; the barber's basins represent a variety of eras and countries. Old convent doors, purchased in Spain at auction, and muted still lifes, further enrich the simplified architecture.*

Miss Trigère had the Fulton Café tables cleaned, which revealed their inlaid marble tops, and joined the tops with an iron base to form a large dining table. The centerpiece is composed of Chinese condiment dishes filled with garden flowers. "The arrangement always stays low, so that vision is not obstructed," Miss Trigère remarks with customary precision. She entertains often; after a leisurely lunch or dinner, guests usually gather in the living room for coffee and stimulating conversation.

ABOVE: *Pauline Trigère's Bedroom is mostly Matisse-inspired. A linen print fabric in the style of the artist suffuses the room with color and pattern. Miss Trigère's fashion dictum applies here: "Fabric is the dictator."*

A canopy bed from New Orleans, with delicate iron tracery, supports generous bedhangings of the same abstract pattern that covers the bed, ceiling and window wall. Though Miss Trigère says her interior designs for La Tortue involved trial and error, creating the bedhangings was a natural expression of her talent: True to the classic tradition of couture, she cuts and drapes direct from the bolt—she does not sketch.

Lightly scaled nineteenth-century bamboo furniture adds to the room's cheerful charm, along with several of the ubiquitous turtles.

117

BELOW: *For a small Guest Bedroom, Miss Trigère had a*
bonnetière *cut in half and upholstered in a floral
chintz based on an old French pattern. The French-born designer
put a conventional bed in between, instead of using an old
Brittany bed, "because old Brittany beds are hard to work
with," she explains. Other European elements elsewhere in the
cozy room are an armoire, made from old French convent doors,
and a Louis XIII desk.*
OPPOSITE: *Miss Trigère's own bold signature fabric
distinctively clothes another Guest Bedroom, which is delineated
by dark wood beams and punctuated with turtle sculptures. An
old school seat that serves as a bench adds a whimsical note to
the spirited design.*

*The vitality and flair that distinguish her fashion designs
find expression throughout Pauline Trigère's home, where
discriminating interiors promote a feeling of ease and
contentment. Though the hostess is a woman of notable elegance,
guests dress casually at La Tortue. "Here in the country, people
don't arrive in their Trigères in the middle of winter," the
designer remarks. "They wear slacks and sweaters. The house
is a good backdrop for such clothes. It is, I think, a rather
pretty country house."*

SONNY AND CHER

Sonny and Cher Bono came a long way together. As their dual career progressed they moved from an apartment in Hollywood to a spacious Bel-Air estate and then to an even more imposing mansion in Holmby Hills, a secluded area of Los Angeles between Bel-Air and Beverly Hills known for its spacious homes and gardens.

Cher had visited the Holmby Hills house when it belonged to Tony Curtis, and had been immediately drawn to it. Built in the 1930s, of Tuscan design, the house is indeed a small palace, and the grounds—with staff quarters, a pool house and a studio—comprise an expansive complement to the main structure. Three gardens, linked by winding paths, become dense woodlands at the boundary of the property. The main residence has more than forty rooms, the principal ones lavishly enhanced with paneling and elaborate moldings.

In Ron Wilson Mr. and Mrs. Bono found a designer dedicated to traditional décor. He had created the interiors for their Bel-Air residence, and when they called on him again he welcomed the opportunity to decorate a house of even more awesome proportions.

From the outside, the Holmby Hills mansions look forbidding to some, but neither the Bonos nor Ron Wilson were overawed. For Sonny and Cher it was a chance to create a setting and life style on a scale commensurate with their stardom; for Mr. Wilson it was an opportunity to engage in what he calls his greatest pleasure—working with fine period furnishings.

"I wasn't going to let it scare me," the designer recalls. "Certain facts had to be accepted. It was a house one could not fight or change in any significant way." Mr. Wilson's concept was to enhance it, to form a union between the needs of the owners and the unalterable thrust of the structure itself.

He does not encourage anyone to follow trends blindly. Too much in the world of modern design, he thinks, suggests transience. A friend once said of Cher Bono, "Old woods and fine design signify permanence to her. She enjoys living among old things that have a history of their own."

Ron Wilson, too, respects historical continuity, gladly accepting the statement of the past. The challenge was to improve on it—to take period pieces and arrange them in a new setting, in order to create a design bridge between the past and the future.

Mr. Wilson completed the interiors within six months. After several brief consultations with Mr. and Mrs. Bono, he went to France and Belgium and Italy, where he found much of the beautiful antique furniture that fills the rooms. He had no formal blueprint, just a carefully planned visual concept in his mind. When the furniture arrived from Europe it fitted exactly.

Indicating the sweeping staircase and imposing crystal chandelier in the entrance hall, he asks rhetorically, "Do you really think three rocks with a glass top would have done anything here?" Mr. Wilson chose to enhance the period paneling with an elaborately carved Régence table and a handmade Portuguese floral rug. The blue-and-white Chinese Export porcelain vase on the table is filled with a burst of long-stemmed silk flowers.

The interiors harmonize completely with the existing background, although each room is interpreted according to its purpose. The grand-scale living room, with its finely detailed paneling, compels a design treatment in context. The rug, with a boldly patterned frieze, and the massing of furniture and objects balance the architectural strength of the room. The designer used muted tones for a harmonious color scheme that would not detract from either the paneling or the furniture.

The palette is brown, beige and slate blue, with accents of gold and soft orange. The large *buffet du corps* on one wall is lined in slate-blue suede, to match the covering on the Louis XVI fireside chairs.

In contrast to the formality of the living room, the oval morning room is a cheery venture into the country. Sofas piled with pillows, and a set of French Provincial spindle-back chairs are covered in a gay floral print, while the parquetry of tabletop and floor are a matching sun-and-zodiac design. Mr. Wilson selected a wrought-iron Tuscan chandelier and scrolled ironwork plant stand to relate to the tracery behind the French doors. The balloon drapery treatment is designed to give a soft look to the impressive architecture.

A less formal look was the concept for the master suite as well. The paneling and molding were painted flat white to subdue their importance, and a French printed cotton, based on an eighteenth-century design, used extensively throughout, became the major theme.

The Italian Renaissance-style bed, with an unusual Louis XV-style carved shell motif ornamented with an eighteenth-century cartouche, is the dramatic focal point of the room. Flanking the Louis XV marble mantel are tall windows with carved floral-wreath arches. The under-drapery is Italian lace. At the other end of the room a Louis XV commode, above which hangs a Venetian mirror, is grouped in classic symmetry with four paintings on black mesh screens.

Cher Bono once observed, in discussing her thoughts about design, "For me, modern furniture has no warmth. I like period rooms, with the richness of age." Mr. Wilson has succeeded in creating an ambience in perfect harmony with the performer's ideal.

ABOVE: *Entertainers Sonny and Cher Bono chose an imposing Tuscan-style estate in the Holmby Hills area of Los Angeles. Iron gates open to the property, which includes a forty-room mansion, built in the 1930s, staff quarters, pool house, studio and three gardens bordered by dense woodland.*

TOP: *French nineteenth-century cherubs greet visitors at the stately brick-and-stone front entrance, announcing the grand scale of the interior. Because Mr. and Mrs. Bono favored traditional décor, they asked designer Ron Wilson to respect and enhance the historical continuity of the structure.*

OPPOSITE: *A sweeping staircase defines the richly paneled Entrance Hall, its delicate iron scrollwork echoed by the pierced carving on the apron of a Régence table. The tapestry-covered chair is also Régence. The rug is Portuguese. Elaborate plaster cornices and marble baseboard moldings add architectural significance, while examples of Chinese Export porcelain—birds, jardiniere and Pilgrim bottles—contribute decorative interest. A Louis XVI tall case clock stands near the archway. Two sparkling crystal chandeliers further the elegant atmosphere.*

LEFT: *A wide vaulted Hallway gives access to the fire-warmed living room. Trompe l'oeil clouds float overhead, punctuated by a Hebraic bronze oil lamp and framed by sculptured plaster cornices. Delicately carved boiserie in the manner of Louis XVI panels the walls, while travertine, partially covered by an Oriental rug, provides the flooring. Furnishings include an elaborate Italian mirror hanging on the wall above a painted Louis XV-style chest.*

ABOVE: *The formal Dining Room continues the aura of traditional refinement. Firelight flickers over Georgian-style pickled oak paneling and glances off the silver and crystal of the tablesetting. An eighteenth-century portrait of a woman is a visual focus above the marble-trimmed fireplace.*

LEFT: *The cheerfully sunlit oval Morning Room takes on a country charm, with a gay floral print fabric wrapping plump sofas and the cushions of Breton spindle-back chairs. The Tuscan chandelier and iron plant stand restate the delicate iron tracery behind the French doors. Unusual balloon drapery in a vivid accent color softens the architecture. The sun-and-zodiac design of the parquetry tabletop are repeated in the wood floor, which is partially covered by a Spanish Savonnerie rug.*

BELOW LEFT: *A paneled hallway arch frames a view of the Dining Room's large-scale appointments; Chinese Export vases on narrow antique oak tables add interest along the way. Upholstered Régence-style chairs attend a massive dining table that expands to accommodate twenty-four. Draperies of tapestry material and a geometric-patterned French needlepoint rug alleviate the expanse of paneling.*

FOLLOWING PAGES: *The vast Living Room easily accommodates a large selection of period furnishings placed to create an effective central conversation area. Soft warm tones and subtle textures enrich the setting, underscored by a custom-designed rug that unifies the color scheme. An eighteenth-century* buffet du corps *on the far wall is lined in the same suede that covers the pair of rare miniature Louis XVI fireside chairs; a French etched and engraved glass fire screen nearby offers protection as well as luminous interest. An elaborate antique cartouche above the mantel, framed by the finely detailed Georgian-style paneling, seems to symbolize the traditional milieu.*

The mood of the Master Suite is lighter, more informal. Paneled walls are painted a flat white to subdue their importance, and a carefree French cotton print fabric, based on an eighteenth-century design, is used extensively throughout.

OPPOSITE: French porcelain lamps with handmade fringed shades stand on draped tables beside the massive Italian Renaissance-style bed. An unusual carved shell motif in the manner of Louis XV distinguishes the bed; above it is an eighteenth-century cartouche.

LEFT: A Louis XV marble mantel surmounts the bronze firebox that casts a special warm glow. Arches of carved floral wreaths delineate the tall windows; the underdrapery is delicate Italian lace.

BELOW LEFT: A balanced arrangement of antique furnishings includes a nineteenth-century Venetian mirror above a Louis XV commode, and a nineteenth-century French slipper chair. The paintings on black mesh screens, and the bronze bust, are eighteenth-century. Deep-toned carpeting, bordered in woven floral needlepoint, complements the upholstery fabric and points up the painstaking attention to detail.

DINAH SHORE

"Some people work their careers around their lives, and some work their lives around their careers. I work my career around my life. My life comes first." The soft southern voice is warm, and the tone positive.

Dinah Shore's life revolves around her home, where she plays tennis, loafs, paints, and entertains a host of friends. This center of fabled hospitality is the result of a multitude of positive decisions made in concert with two talented men: interior designer Val Arnold and architect Edward Grenzbach.

Miss Shore had heard about the architect through a friend. "I went over to see a house he had built. The lot was just nothing, but he had done some enchanting things. Many architects build houses, but when I saw that house I thought: 'This is a *home.'*"

Miss Shore and the architect looked at houses everywhere. "There was always something that could be done to each one. We would look at each other and say, 'What do you think? Will a tennis court fit on this lot?'"

One day they heard about a house on a lot big enough for *two* tennis courts. Miss Shore bought it that afternoon, even though the house was big and dark. The living room was like a hall, but the floor plan basically suited her needs and the house was structurally sound.

It was a question of what improvements had to be made. Miss Shore moved in with her children and her housekeeper of many years, Pauline Berman, and lived there through the six months of remodeling.

"We made tremendous structural changes," she says. "The patios came first, and then the garden room, which now overlooks the pool and tennis court."

"The living room was just normal size," Mr. Grenzbach recalls, "but Dinah's such a space filler, we needed to add the area that now constitutes the garden room. The addition has a brick floor and a pitched ceiling up to a big gable and fixed wood sash, with large panes of glass. It's now a dramatic extroverted room, yet with the paned windows and the white trim, it's very traditional."

Miss Shore adds, "Every room has its own personality and theme and mood, and that's so important to me. We did the foyer and hallways, and fooled around a little bit with the basic shape of the dining room, too. We changed the existing bedrooms and closets, and lastly, built a little guest house in the back."

A noted cook, and author of two cookbooks, Dinah Shore considers the kitchen an integral part of her life. Accordingly, the architect and the interior designer reshaped the existing space by combining pantry, kitchen, breakfast nook, laundry and utility room into one kitchen area. The arched used-brick hood above the range, and the wood ceiling in the dining alcove nearby suggest an English cottage. To make room for the beams and hood, the architect pushed the ceiling into some idle attic space, creating a canopy effect.

Miss Shore's proud claim is that every inch of space has been used to the best advantage: "Behind every mirror, every wall hanging, there is storage space. Even the television is set into the wall behind a painting."

Dinah Shore met Val Arnold a few years ago when he designed a house for friends of hers. "I was so happy when I found Val, because he says, 'Okay, if you don't like that, here's something else.'" She continues: "Good designers begin to sense the way you feel, the way you react. It's a special sensitivity, an intuition, really."

If something didn't fit, and Miss Shore was reluctant to part with it, adjustments were made. She points to the dining room table: "It is really too large for the room, but I love it and wanted to keep it. Val said, 'If you're going to have an overpowering table, then the chairs have to do something.'" Mr. Arnold's solution was to remove the tortoiseshell finish from the chairs and have them lacquered a vivid shade. "I wanted more levity," he explains, "because the table is so serious."

Val Arnold submitted colors and fabrics for the study/screening room in American Indian motifs, soft tones of the plains and deserts. An Indian rug used as a wall hanging conceals the glass behind which two 16-mm. projectors function in a small adjoining room.

Dinah Shore is a collector, but she doesn't collect art for investment purposes. "I know when art pleases my eye, just as there are some people it gives me great pleasure to look at. It's like the dining room table—I know it's foolish to keep it, but I'm the one who lives here. Something special happens when you encounter an object that really speaks to you—maybe it's a painting, a piece of furniture, a plant. I never get tired of looking at my paintings. Plants are very special. Even if you had nothing else in a house except plants, somehow you'd have a place you could call home."

Dinah Shore's home opens to hospitality on every side. It can accommodate four people or twenty-four—although such a large group is definitely an exception. "On winter evenings, when there are only a couple of us, we'll light a fire and eat in the alcove, or perhaps at the low table in the living room or in the garden room. Or sometimes in the screening room. You can dine anywhere in this house—even in the bedroom!"

Miss Shore does most of the cooking herself. "I'll have friends for an early dinner, and we'll sit around talking and having a marvelous time until two or three in the morning. There's one way I can always tell when a house really works—when people don't want to leave."

ABOVE: *Dinah Shore is an enthusiastic tennis player, so when she found a house with enough property for* **two** *tennis courts, she bought it immediately. An exterior view of the Beverly Hills residence focuses on the gabled and glass-walled garden room addition, which faces an expanse of verdant lawn.*

OPPOSITE: *Sunlight floods the Garden Room, set for informal dining. Light-painted beams, brick flooring and paned windows create an informal greenhouse atmosphere in this high-ceilinged room. Lush greenery and floral-patterned upholstery echo the view of the carefully tended landscaping.*

OPPOSITE: *In the Living Room, plants and flowers accent comfortable, large-scale upholstered pieces covered in deep-toned linen velour. The glow from the black marble fireplace appointed with French Empire andirons is reflected in the polished finish of the lacquered, textured table. The painting on the right wall moves on a hinge to reveal a television set.*

ABOVE: *This versatile space serves as a Study, and also as a Screening Room when the Indian rug on the far wall is lowered to reveal projection equipment in an adjoining room. Butcher-block cube tables on casters were custom designed to separate for flexible use. Indian rugs and baskets and coiled-rope table lamps add to the American Indian feeling.*

The Dining Room table sparkles with Bohemian-overlay
stemware and antique English silverware. The walls are
upholstered, with gracefully rounded corners trimmed in fabric
that coordinates with the window valance, visible in the mirror.
The window treatment fabric is a print based on an
eighteenth-century French pattern. Miss Shore wanted the
room designed around her large mahogany table. A
nineteenth-century Chinese ginger jar with carved-wood top
serves as the centerpiece, and an aged Buddha watches from the
sideboard, amid cascading greenery.

"I have been gathering and trying out recipes ever since I can remember," says Dinah Shore, whose cooking talent has been shared in her television shows and cookbooks. The large country-style Kitchen was created from a cluster of small conventional rooms. The ceiling was raised to make room for exposed wooden beams and an arched used-brick hood over the range. Boards of Douglas fir create a rustic canopy over the nineteenth-century French table in an alcove.

Well-used pans hanging above the shining stainless-steel range announce that the kitchen is very much a working room, for all its warmth and charm. Behind the range is a ceramic tile wall, which continues the brick pattern. In the background on the right, glass-enclosed shelves separate cabinets of natural plantation pecan. Elsewhere in the kitchen are bookcases to hold Miss Shore's collection of more than three hundred cookbooks.

BOB NEWHART

One afternoon Mr. and Mrs. Bob Newhart were driving home along a winding Bel-Air lane unfamiliar to them. Suddenly Ginnie Newhart cried, "Stop the car!"

"I thought we must have hit something," Bob Newhart recalls. "I slammed on the brakes, and Ginnie said, 'There's my dream house.' "

Ginnie Newhart continued to dream, and then some months later she learned that the property was for sale. The Newharts lost no time in buying the Brittany-style home that had charmed them both.

"We were both ready for a change," Mrs. Newhart remembers. "Bob remarked one day that we hadn't sat down in our living room for years. Even our den was so vast that we never felt like relaxing or putting our feet up. We used to retreat to our bedroom early every evening because it was the only spot where we felt at home."

Now the television star, his wife, three children and three dogs are comfortably settled. But it was a precipitous change, and intensive work followed.

When designers Phyllis Cole Rowen and Robert Dawson Mentzer were called in, the new house was in escrow. Because the owner was still in residence, the Newharts and their designers were limited to one visit.

"We rushed in," Mr. Mentzer recalls, "talking ninety miles an hour, and made notes as fast as we could. Bob had brought his camera and snapped pictures right and left. We ordered papers, fabrics and carpets just from our notes, the photographs, and what we remembered."

"The house is beautiful, architecturally," Mrs. Rowen comments. "But much of the interior detail had been obscured or misused. We brought it back to its original condition, finding the things that had been pulled away from the country look and restoring them."

Much was there already—leaded windows, bookcases, moldings; but the moldings were painted red. The designers stripped and repainted them and upholstered the walls to emphasize the beautiful detail. The dadoes were sponged, for an antique effect.

The décor is a mix of Country French and English, chosen to complement the house and create the informal look the Newharts prefer. Robert Mentzer recalls, "It was an old house, built in the 1930s by Gerard R. Colcord, and a period design as well, so we wanted everything to look right. Ginnie has a marvelous collection of Steuben—inspired by a gift from Ethel Kennedy—and she wanted it displayed in the dining room. The cabinets had to be custom designed. You can't find antique cabinets just this high and that deep and that wide."

Traditional furnishings in the living room are complemented by a Portuguese needlepoint rug. In the den a massive cabinet in the style of Louis XV houses the television set. The custom bar was constructed of two antique English apothecary chests joined by the mirrored section of a pub door. Intermixed with Daumier lithographs is a collection of personal memorabilia: Mr. Newhart's treasured Peabody Award, his gold records, and a personal letter from President John F. Kennedy.

When the designers began working on the house, Mrs. Newhart was just beginning to develop a love of antiques. She had already acquired a number of vintage telephones—a happy reminder of the telephone monologues that launched her husband's career. Mrs. Rowen and Mr. Mentzer encouraged her new bent.

Ginnie Newhart is frank about her past experiences with designers: "They always inflicted things on me that I didn't like, and when I wouldn't go along with them they would lose interest. But with Phyllis and Robert, if I didn't like something, they'd find an alternative."

"When we were first doing the house," the designers remember, "we would gather everything together and then show Bob, in one meeting. Ginnie wanted him to know what was going on. We found that what would please Ginnie would generally please Bob."

But Mr. Newhart had strong intuitive likes and dislikes, and there were times when he balked. "One type of décor I cannot live with is Chinese," he says, "although I love French. One day I came home and found this Chinese fabric on the living room couches. Everyone kept telling me it was *chinoiserie*—a French word for an Oriental look. I chuckled, but I gave in. For a long time I've had the feeling that I'm the only sane person in the world anyway. So when I run into the situation where I think it's Chinese and everybody else insists that it's French, I'm conditioned to accept it."

A similar confrontation took place when Mr. Newhart had his first look at the master bedroom, with intricate leafy patterns covering the sofa and climbing the walls. Butterflies had been painted on the ceiling, for what the designers call "a total look." "I thought it was too feminine," Bob Newhart remarks. "Then I had a lot of people, mainly my wife, telling me it wasn't. Anyway, I've become used to it. I'm one of the great adjusters.

"Our old house was so large we used to have to invite thirty people, just to fill up the space," he recalls wryly. "I never had a chance to talk to anyone."

But in this well-coordinated house, while there is ample room for larger groups, intimate conversational gatherings of four or six are not lost in vast spaces. To the lasting delight of the Newharts, there is no communication gap—which is just as it should be, for the home of a man whose name is a famous one in the field of communications.

The beguiling storybook façade of Mr. and Mrs. Bob Newhart's Bel-Air residence immediately attracted them. Built in 1932, by Gerard R. Colcord, the gabled, 6,500-square-foot Brittany-style structure represents a cozier atmosphere for the Newhart family than their previous large and formal Beverly Hills home. A circular driveway, luxuriantly edged with foliage, approaches the house, which is set far back from a winding hillside road. Informal masses of plants, blooming in simple clay pots at the entrance, prepare visitors for the warm colorful interiors.

The Newharts enlisted the skills of designers Phyllis Cole Rowen and Robert Dawson Mentzer to restore architectural details that had been obscured over the years and to initiate new construction. Since the Newharts have three young children, the pool was fenced as soon as they moved in. In order to simplify family living during the year-long project, the painting and papering were coordinated to dovetail with interior architectural work in each area of the house.

Country French and English appointments complement the Living Room architecture. Dark wood tones and a vivid mixture of patterns and textures pervade the 18-by-29-foot room, underscored by Portuguese needlepoint and French linen-velvet rugs.

"I didn't want a showcase, where you were afraid to sit down," says Bob Newhart. Ginnie Newhart recalls: "When I was a girl, growing up in Virginia, I practically never saw the inside of our formal living room until I was about twelve. I'd rather have people be comfortable, put their feet up and not feel hysterical if they spill something." Period accessories include Venetian mirrors, French tôle jardinieres and an Oriental bronze lamp base.

141

The Newharts appreciate the smaller size of their Den, finding
it warm and inviting for evening relaxation. Checked wall
upholstery sparked by pristine beams and molding coordinates
with other fresh fabrics and a French needlepoint rug. Enriching
the setting are books and memorabilia, including the Peabody
Award and two gold records.

ABOVE LEFT: *Because the Newharts enjoy the conviviality of a bar, Mrs. Rowen and Mr. Mentzer designed one and had it built from two English apothecary cabinets joined by the mirrored section of a pub door. The custom cabinet behind the bar holds a framed letter from President John F. Kennedy, glassware and a variety of collectables, including part of a vintage telephone collection. Sharing wall space is a Daumier lithograph Mrs. Newhart found at auction, and a mirrored cigarette sign, which celebrates Ginnie Newhart's name and birthplace.*
ABOVE: *The Dining Room is a more formal statement, illuminated by a gleaming crystal chandelier. A custom pine cabinet, one of a pair, displays a portion of Mrs. Newhart's Steuben glass collection, initiated some years ago by the gift of a Steuben ashtray from Mrs. Robert F. Kennedy. A framed eighteenth-century Sèvres plate, handpainted and signed, adorns an upholstered wall; the English server is also eighteenth century. Painted dentil molding and a leaded bay window contribute to the country cottage charm.*

GORE VIDAL

Gore Vidal—novelist, playwright, critic and political commentator—has been called "the last gentleman of American letters." "I am a 100 percent American writer," he affirms, "which is probably why I live abroad so much of the time." In his Italian villa, *La Rondinaia,* on a cliff high over the Gulf of Salerno, Mr. Vidal feels a part of the American expatriate artistic tradition.

From Ravello, the approach to La Rondinaia—"The Swallow's Nest"—can be made only on foot. There is no other way. The labyrinthine walks of the old town suddenly give way to a narrow path leading through olive trees, black cypresses and colorful masses of flowers, both wild and cultivated.

The villa itself is not immediately visible, but glimpses of it can be seen through the trees. Below, terraced vineyards and lemon groves stretch to the sea, with an infinity of blue in the distance. A pair of stone lions guards the entrance, and in a niche above the door is a stone image of Saint Catherine; the deep silence is broken only by the singing of birds.

Inside La Rondinaia Gore Vidal explains why he has chosen this particular part of Italy. "A number of years ago I received a questionnaire from a magazine, asking me what I thought was the most beautiful place in the world. I answered, 'Ravello.'"

This venerable village was once a thriving city of palaces and churches, built by the merchant princes of Amalfi, but the population was decimated by plague in the fifteenth century. Many who survived the plague left the stricken city and never returned.

"In 1972, when I was looking for a country place in Italy," continues Mr. Vidal, "I saw this one advertised in an Italian publication. After one look I took it on a lease and bought six extra acres. The property is mostly planted to lemons, but there are olives, chestnuts and grapes, too, and we have our own wine and olive oil. I sell the lemons and grow my own vegetables, including American sweet corn.

"Although not old by Italian standards, the house has a colorful history. La Rondinaia was built in 1927, by Countess Szechenyi, the daughter of Lord Grimthorpe. His house, *Villa Cimbrone,* overlooks mine. The countess wanted to prove that anything her father could do, she could do better. The house was built by a local engineer, not an architect, and is almost a miracle of construction. It literally clings to a rocky cliff face that rises a thousand feet sheer from the sea.

"In the thirties Stokowski and Greta Garbo stayed here, and later, Princess Ercolani. During World War II it was a rest home for British army officers.

"I've made very few structural changes. What I like about the house is that it follows the classical Roman plan, with a series of rooms opening off long halls. The fireplaces, made of tufa and local ceramic tile, are typical of this area. I opened the wall between the living room and the dining room and built one fireplace. I bought very little furniture, simply re-covering what was already here. Bill Willis, the interior designer, came up from his home in Marrakech to do the living room, and he brought the Moroccan rugs with him. He designed the big low table and took the colors for its mosaic top from the eleventh-century Basilica of Ravello. We found those big oil jars up on the hill. We cleaned them up and filled them with dried grasses."

Sometimes Mr. Vidal writes in bed or lounging on a sofa. At other times he works at the desk in the study. Several of his best-selling novels were written in this serene and attractive room. "The study is a wonderful place to work," he comments.

The villa is also a wonderful place in which to relax. There are perhaps few places in the world more enchanting—and more soothing to the spirit—than this particular part of Italy, rich in history and the acceptance of life. The aura of the countryside brings with it peace and a heightened enjoyment of pleasures often curtailed or forgotten in northern climates: such pleasures as long leisurely dinners and that vanishing art, the give-and-take of good conversation.

On summer evenings La Rondinaia is often the scene of small dinner parties, which begin at eight or nine o'clock. Women guests, wearing long, flowing gowns, step gingerly along the garden path, evening slippers held in their hands. The walk is well worth it; dinner wines come from the villa's own vineyards, and the cuisine is excellent. Howard Austen, who takes care of manorial matters so that Mr. Vidal can devote himself to writing, is companion, secretary, majordomo, head gardener—and a superbly inventive cook.

And as one would expect, the dinner conversation, led by Mr. Vidal, is witty and entertaining. There is music after dinner, impromptu dancing and more talk. On such evenings the living room is bathed in a soft light that plays on the vaulted ceilings, slowly fading as it descends. It sheds a benevolent glow on everyone; the women seem more beautiful, and the men more handsome in its gentle radiance.

Mr. Vidal is the center of a civilized world in La Rondinaia, a world perfectly attuned to his work and pleasure. "I've had really great luck," he once observed. "I do exactly what I want to do and I've made a living, which you're not supposed to be able to do if you write the way you want to."

SCAVULLO

145

BELOW: *From a balcony of his enchanting seaside villa* La Rondinaia—*"The Swallow's Nest"—high above the Italian village of Ravello, writer Gore Vidal enjoys a spectacular view of the glorious Mediterranean coastline as it conforms to the Gulf of Salerno.*

LOWER LEFT: *Stone lions guard the entrance to the poetic retreat, which can be reached only by a rustic footpath through tall trees and bright wild flowers.*

LOWER RIGHT: *Glass entrance doors, overlaid with wrought-iron tracery, open to the large terrace.*

BELOW: *Roman arches along a portion of terrace exemplify the villa's classic architecture as they frame the expansive view. Mr. Vidal leased the house after one look, then bought six acres of property just below it. The land is chiefly planted to lemons, with a few olive and chestnut trees. He grows vegetables and grapes, also; guests savor the white and rosé wines made from grapes grown in his terraced vineyards. Secluded from all but the blue of sea and sky, the villa provides the author with a perfect setting for both relaxation and inspiration.*

BELOW: *Above the Living Room's tufa fireplace, a painting by Parneo extends the Romanesque ambience. The 22-by-32-foot room, divided by an archway, is appointed for casual comfort. A cool neutral-toned cotton covers large-scale upholstered pieces and drapes the interesting arched windows. Ceramic tile flooring is covered with woven straw overlaid with Moroccan rugs brought from Marrakech by designer Bill Willis.*
LOWER LEFT AND CENTER: *"What I like about the house," says Mr. Vidal, "is that it follows the classical Roman plan: a series of rooms opening off long halls." At the end of the Hallway a graceful wrought-iron door contrasts with thick white walls.*
LOWER RIGHT: *The focal point of another Living Room view is the large low table Mr. Willis designed and had made in Rome; the colors of its mosaic top were taken from the eleventh-century Basilica of Ravello. Once a prosperous city built by the merchant princes of Amalfi, Ravello was decimated by a fifteenth-century plague and never regained its economic stature.*

Music and impromptu dancing follow dinner on pleasurable summer evenings at La Rondinaia. Sound equipment is concealed in the antique cabinet. While the architectural lighting is soft and unobtrusive, the conversation is always stimulating and often challenging. A fifteen-foot vaulted ceiling easily accepts the few monumental indigenous ornaments: "We found those big oil jars up on the hill and filled them with dried grasses," explains Mr. Vidal, who calls Ravello "the most beautiful place in the world."

LEFT: *With the wit and perception for which he is well known, Mr. Vidal engages dinner guests in spirited, sometimes iconoclastic, discussion. The Dining Room trestle table and credenza date from the sixteenth century, while the mirror adds a Baroque touch. The painting of a Roman head is by Pollitzer.*

LEFT CENTER: *Howard Austen's simplified Bedroom features an Italian wrought-iron bed. Mr. Austen handles the management of the residence, freeing Mr. Vidal to write such best-sellers as* Burr *and* 1876, *and to function as a critic and essayist.*

BELOW LEFT: *A gilded Rococo marble-topped Hallway console, arranged with an equally elaborate mirror and pair of sconces, stands ready to serve as a way station for a casual hat or a good book.*

Mr. Vidal's large Bedroom is a Spartan statement, defined by a twelve-foot vaulted ceiling and a fireplace of tufa and ceramic tile—all typical of the locale. The suite of gold-decorated painted-wood furniture once belonged to Jenny Lind. An architectural engraving depicts the author's former Greek Revival-style home in Barrytown, New York; the Morris rocking chair is a memento from that house. Family portraits further personalize the atmosphere, which Mr. Vidal finds conducive to work as well as to relaxation and rest.

ROBERT REDFORD

The first thing that greets a visitor in the entrance hall of the sleek Fifth Avenue apartment is an inchworm. Not the garden variety, but the red plastic kind with wheels, which four-year-olds pedal furiously up and down New York sidewalks. The inchworm, along with the guitar slung in the corner of a boy's bedroom and pink satin ballet shoes tacked to a girl's bedroom door, announce an active family household, the Manhattan home of Robert Redford, his wife, Lola, and their three children.

Mr. Redford has called their house in Utah "the last bastion." "And the apartment is our fortress in the city," says Lola Redford. "Yes, this is where we hole up," agrees her husband. He has just arrived from Utah, where he has been planting alfalfa. The 1,100-acre ranch in the Wasatch mountains is where they spend much of the summer. But New York is where the Redfords settled after their marriage, more than a decade and a half ago. Because their children are enrolled in local schools, and for the sake of old friendships, they divide their time between Manhattan and the mountains.

"As a family," says Mrs. Redford, "we have a firm belief in roots, and we have them here. We feel that's very important today. Our romance with New York never fades. We love the area where we live. It's quiet, out of the way and we can walk around in our jeans."

"New York is dirty, frightening and violent, but it is also the most honest city in the United States. I couldn't live without it," Mr. Redford adds. "One of the disadvantages of living here is that you can lose a sense of space. I have a feeling of confinement every so often. That's why I've always felt you must create an escape."

At home, privacy and comfort are paramount. "Being married as long as we have been, and having lived in different places, you develop an instinct about whether you're comfortable or not," explains Lola Redford.

"I think a house should be like an old suit," her husband adds. "It should conform to the body."

They prefer to furnish their homes themselves. "I don't see decorating as doing a series of rooms," Mrs. Redford comments. "I think your inner self and where you live are somehow connected."

"Lola and I are interested in all aspects of design and architecture," Mr. Redford adds. "We find tremendous stimulation from a creative effort we've made together."

When Mr. Redford was doing the rock superstructure for the house in Utah, he asked an Indian to give him a key to arranging the rocks. The Hopi replied, "What key? Just look around you. Did anybody arrange the rocks in that mountain?" Robert Redford says he is as proud of that rockwork as of anything he's done.

"We wanted to create an indoor/outdoor atmosphere in the apartment," Mr. Redford continues. "We appreciate the East and the West, but we didn't want to make too much contrast. I can't live without a western touch; it's too much a part of me. But then, in our house in Utah we have a number of urban touches, too."

Lola Redford, who was born in Utah, is quick to agree. To illustrate the way they mix city and country life she mentions the time she and her husband drove a carload of sagebrush back to Manhattan.

"There it is in the hall," she says. "Don't you smell it?" Their expansive and airy eight-room apartment is warmed with earth colors, natural textures and western artifacts: wooden beams and paneling, paintings of Indians, by Ira Yeager, trees in straw baskets, a glass case of rare Kachina dolls, pottery done by an Indian friend, and a nostalgic poster of the motion picture *Butch Cassidy and the Sundance Kid.*

"What we're trying to do is preserve our heritage," he points out. "These are all part of Lola's heritage." He indicates a collection of objects from Mormon pioneer cabins. "We've lived in this city during periods of great sorrow and happiness; with money and without money; and what we like to have around us now are meaningful nonmaterialistic things." Lola Redford reaches for a bronze statue of a cowboy on a horse, an award her husband received for making a movie about mountain man Jeremiah Johnson: "Isn't this gorgeous?"

The elongated living room, where the Redfords are sitting on a saddle-brown sofa, doubles as a screening room when they entertain.

Between the living room and the family bedrooms is a cozy book-lined study filled with plaid furniture. One wall is studded with framed photographs of her husband with former Mayor John Lindsay, with Barbra Streisand, with the *Butch Cassidy* cast, with his Texas grandmother. "This is our private room, where Bob reads scripts, where I work on my projects and where we argue about whose desk this is," Lola Redford says, as she serves rose hip tea and honey. Looking thoughtfully around the room, she sums up her feelings about their New York home and her responsibilities as the decorator: "Our house isn't perfect, nor is it finished. I know I shouldn't have bought that rug or this sofa—which somehow looked different when I picked it out. The mistakes are mine, but I don't mind. Striving for perfection, especially in something as subjective as a home, is an American hang-up. I think about what John Denver said to me: 'Perfection has nothing to do with not making mistakes.' I like that."

Robert Redford agrees. "Everything we do is something of a search. It's not important to find what you're looking for. It's the effort that's exciting."

Mr. and Mrs. Robert Redford and their three children divide
their time between Manhattan and the mountains of Utah,
savoring the best of each very different environment. In summer
they spread out on a 1,100-acre ranch in the Wasatch
mountains, where they backpack, ride horses and cruise Lake
Powell in a houseboat. During the school year their life is more
compact; they settle snugly into an eight-room upper Fifth
Avenue apartment. "This is where we hole up," says
actor/producer Redford, for whom privacy is paramount.
OPPOSITE: A large sectional sofa in the Living Room offers the
kind of casual comfort the Redfords enjoy. Mrs. Redford
designed the glass-and-wood coffee table. Says her husband:
"Percentagewise, this house is Lola's effort, as she and the
children are here more than I am. But Lola and I have a
similar approach to the use of space, so it works well for both of
us." The large jug was made by Navajo friend Lucy Leuppe;
the bronze cowboy on horseback was awarded to Robert
Redford for the film Jeremiah Johnson.
ABOVE: A collection of photographs of family and friends, and
pictures of Mr. Redford on various movie locations cover a
wall in the deep-toned Study. Daughter Shauna Redford
sculpted the clay dog on the table. Contemporary artist Ira
Yeager painted the coyote, as well as the large American Indian
portraits in other rooms.

OPPOSITE: *Warm wood tones mellow an uncluttered Dining Room. "We enjoy entertaining at home," says Robert Redford. "Not as social events; rather, as private gatherings of friends." An evening at the Redford home might include dinner for eight to twelve guests and afterwards a movie screened in the living room. "I usually cook," says Lola Redford, "and Bob makes a salad or his fantastic yogurt."*

RIGHT: *Intriguing wooden ceremonial Kachina dolls, made by the Hopi tribe, are souvenirs of the Redfords' many visits to Indian reservations in the West. Mrs. Redford designed the contemporary glass-and-wood display case.*

Lola and Robert Redford mix their city and country lives effectively: they take urban touches to the mountains and they bring engaging western artifacts to the metropolis, which has been the family's home base for many years.

The Redfords take great interest in architecture and design—they built their glass-and-cedar triple-A-frame home in Utah—and prefer to create their own interior designs. "We get tremendous stimulation from a creative effort we've made together," Robert Redford remarks. For their comfortable city spaces they chose wood beams and paneling, earth tones and natural textures to establish a feeling of the West, which has always been so important to the family.

157

BARBARA WALTERS

Barbara Walters is famous in a way that has only become possible in the twentieth century. Her electronic presence is part of a daily ritual in millions of homes across the country, and the intelligence and charisma she projects have made her a personality in her own right. Her home functions as a private haven, an expression of a dynamic and creative spirit.

The private life of Barbara Walters is centered in one of those old New York buildings distinguished for unostentatious elegance and strategic location. "My friends keep telling me I should move to the East Side and buy a penthouse and live up to my image," she says. "But that doesn't interest me.

"This is a big old comfortable building, and it's an old, comfortable apartment. What I like most about it is that it has a very warm easy look. It's not a 'decorated' apartment. Designer Burt Wayne is an old friend, and what he did was to come in and kind of pull it together. For instance, in the living room are black-and-white slipcovers. I had red couches, and they became rather shabby, so I put the slipcovers on for the summer. Burt said, 'You'll love them, and won't take them off.' He was right—and since then we have kept black-and-white slipcovers on, all the year round."

Burt Wayne, of Wayne and Doktor, Ltd., is a relaxed and urbane man who has the kind of supportive personality so vital in dealing with people who have demanding schedules. "Barbara has a grueling pace to keep up," Mr. Wayne points out, "and while she is intensely interested in everything around her, she simply didn't have much time to spend on the details of her new home. That's where I came in!"

Mr. Wayne, an old friend of Miss Walters, sums up his approach to design: "There are several important factors. The most important is knowing the client well enough to sense when he or she is ready for a change," he says. "A unified sensibility is absolutely vital, of course, and a certain tenacity, as well.

"I think it's important for clients to be involved," Mr. Wayne insists, "to be interested in how an eighteenth-century chair can be made to work in a modern environment. On the other hand, a designer has to take taste and personality into full account. This apartment was a particular challenge, because Barbara is such a complex and productive person, with so many different needs."

Each room is a smooth blending of the Wayne approach and Miss Walters' preference for objects with personal associations. "Take the living room, for example," says Burt Wayne. "I worked with a lot of Barbara's things. The rug is from Iran—she bought it when she went there to interview the Shah—and the pots and cups on the low table are objects that Moshe Dayan gave her from his own collection of antiquities. On the other hand, the gray walls, the black-and-white motif on the sofas are my concepts. You see, it's all in how you hold it together. In this case, such serene classics of modern design as the chairs by Charles Eames and Mies van der Rohe become very important. They are the touchstones in a room, the grace notes of timelessness, which give a rich dimension to design."

Miss Walters adds, "Many of the things in the apartment were my mother's and father's, some of the nicest things, as a matter of fact. I like best the lovely old pieces like the crystal candelabra in the dining room."

"Barbara, as we all know, is a great conversationalist," Mr. Wayne says, "so I conceived the dining room to provide an intimate atmosphere; Barbara doesn't really care for large groups. But for the occasions when the number of guests exceeds eight or ten, I had another table made, which can be folded away and brought out again when it's needed."

Typical Wayne details, such as the contrasting mood of the Thonet chairs matched against the steel-and-glass buffet, and the careful integration of Victoriana, round off the sparkling, yet warm room.

The bedroom evokes a completely different mood. Here, country reigns—floral patterns bloom on walls, cushions and chaise, echoed by bowls of cut flowers on tables. It was originally designed as an upbeat eye-opener during the years when Miss Walters began each working day at 5:00 A.M. Now it is a favorite place to return to after long days and frequent travels.

According to Mr. Wayne, "It is Barbara's refuge, a place for her to get away from the high-pressure atmosphere of the studio."

"My greatest pleasure is to curl up with a book," Miss Walters confides. "I'm absolutely in love with my apartment," she goes on. "It's just—peace. It's also surprisingly flexible. I find I can entertain here very well for a few people or as many as thirty.

"The great thing about working with Burt is the fact that he never makes me feel as if I have to throw anything away. He's very sane when it comes to what people own and cherish. I have pieces of furniture that I am sure many designers would have wanted me to get rid of, but Burt patiently worked them into the new space. Working with him has been a growth process for me. I've learned to be a good deal more conscious of my day-to-day environment. Whenever I want to buy something new, he'll say 'No—because one of these days we have to do the whole place over.' But you know, I doubt that we will. I'm happy with my home just the way it is."

The Living Room of Barbara Walters' Manhattan apartment exhibits the use of modern lines and a simplified color scheme to create a timeless environment in which conversation flows freely and the most cherished objects are those of personal significance.

RIGHT: *Shades of black and white predominate, especially in a corner conducive to games and reading. Designer Burt Wayne used velvet draperies and a floor-length table covering to counterpoint smooth contemporary chair and lamp curves. Two antique Chinese bronze cranes bow gracefully from atop the table; they were given to Barbara Walters by her parents. On rare occasions when the guest list is large this table becomes an auxiliary dining table. As a general rule, Miss Walters entertains small groups, because she feels that conversation flourishes in a more intimate gathering.*

OPPOSITE: *Originally only a summer solution for sofas scheduled to be reupholstered, bold vine-patterned slipcovers have become year-round staples of the design. Plump pillows repeat the achromatic contrast in differing motifs. The successful blending of the décor with personalized objects is typified by the use of a rug purchased by Miss Walters while in Iran to interview the Shah. Another illustrious interview subject, Israel's Moshe Dayan, gifted her with the pottery jugs and bowls, dating from 1500 B.C., which are displayed on the low square table.*

Memorabilia on the table between the sofas affirm their owner's wide-ranging interests and professional travels: a lump of coal she dug out of a Welsh mine wall; a tall, carved ivory ball-within-a-ball from China; medals from Romania and Israel; a carved turtle from Spain; antique perfume bottles from Egypt and an ivory-inlaid Persian box. An Alexander Calder lithograph edges the room with a patch of dancing color, and potted plants at varying heights add a verdant natural touch to the cosmopolitan mode.

Shirred wall fabric, restated by a fringed glass-topped table
drape, is primarily responsible for the Dining Room's intimate
atmosphere. The balanced arrangement is light in scale,
proportion and tone. An antique Venetian mirror and romantic
heirloom crystal candelabra complement crisp glass-and-chrome
serving tables. The plate on a stand was a gift from the Shah of
Iran, at the 2,500th anniversary celebration of the Persian
empire; the Waterford crystal bowl was presented to Miss
Walters by the Ireland-United States Council.

RIGHT AND BELOW RIGHT: *Barbara Walters'*
Bedroom is as vital as her talent, offering her a light
cheerful setting for the rare private moments in her
busy schedule, when she can reflect, relax and
recharge. A bower of multicolored tulips blooms on
walls, table and chaise longue. Plants, vases of fresh
flowers and stacks of books share table surfaces, as
they do elsewhere in the apartment.

"This is Barbara's refuge," says designer
Wayne, "away from the glare of arc lights and the
high-pressure atmosphere of the studio." A group of
small boxes on the bedside table indicates Miss
Walters' interest in collecting mementos of her travels.

JEAN KERR

We are agreed that a house should have that "lived-in" look. But lived in by *whom*? After years of benign neglect our house was beginning to look like one of those small off-season resort hotels that cater to transient students. Since that was precisely what we did cater to, one could see a certain logic in the situation. One could also see parts of the old slipcovers emerging through the "new" slipcovers on the sofa. But the status might have remained forever quo if my mother hadn't come to visit. One thing my mother has never learned is that when dealing with a thorny situation one should find a bush and beat about it. Consequently, after the first harmonious five minutes, she declared that the house was a disaster area and that I was a mess. Or that *may* have been vice versa. In any event, I could see that for the greater glory of Larchmont, *steps* would have to be taken.

So, choosing the larger of the two evils, *slightly* larger, I decided to redecorate the downstairs. However, because I was going into rehearsal with a play and had to select actors, I knew I couldn't attempt the much more difficult chore of choosing fabrics. I typically select fabrics by picking up twenty-three books of samples (no, no, not all at the same time), and I keep them propped open by weighting them with telephone books (Manhattan directories are ideal for the purpose) under a reading light. And then I stare at each sample soulfully as though I were Elvira Madigan taking a long last look at the beloved. My problem is that I can see that three large, slightly berserk pink peonies look rather stunning on a swatch of moss green linen but I can't imagine (maybe I don't want to) the infinity of lunatic blossoms that would be required to cover a large sofa. For this and other reasons, I decided to hire an interior designer.

F. Wayne Stellmacher had been recommended to me as brave, reverent, prompt and accomplished, and as possessing, in addition, the soothing qualities of a good obstetrician. I didn't learn until sometime later that he had just finished designing all the interiors of a large national bank—a fact that my friends found hilarious. "Great, you can put a teller's cage in the front hall and pay the kids their allowances properly." My friends have lived to repent the error of their jokes.

Phyllis McGinley has written that you should buy nothing that you don't know to be useful or believe to be beautiful. This has always made perfect sense to me, which made it difficult to explain some of the objects in my living room (the room that was). Of course that armchair was definitely useful when we bought it secondhand for thirteen dollars, in the first year we were married. But what about the footstool that never did match anything and was too low to put your feet on?

In any case, life with a designer was a little different from what I had imagined. I had supposed it would be like using the yellow section of the phone book, where "your fingers do the walking." As it turned out, I did more walking than at any time since my first visit to Venice, where I was slow to observe that there really *were* no taxis. Together Wayne and I climbed flights of stairs to fourth floor lofts, where five or six pieces of furniture stood stark and beautiful in white muslin.

We also rode in sleek silent elevators to the top floors of fabric houses, where enough material was on display to cover every piece of furniture on the North American continent, including pianos.

Wayne would march purposefully to the section that contained "fabrics we are looking for"; I would just disappear into the first set of swiveling racks. It was in this retreat that I was actually of some help one afternoon. I was standing absolutely still, clutching my carpet sample and my memories, when a woman beside me announced with real excitement, "Henry, that's exactly what I want for my sun porch—that red and green plaid." Since there was nothing but antique satins for yards around, it dawned on me that what had caught her eye was the caftan I was wearing. So it was no surprise when, a moment later, a distinguished-looking gentleman asked me where I had purchased this garment!

One advantage of shopping with a designer is that you get such special, such thoughtful consideration from the showroom. We had finally selected a handsome crewel fabric for the living room, and I asked the man in charge, "How do you clean this?" He lowered his already low voice and whispered, "In India, they wash it in the river." Well, that cleared up everything. "Of course," I said. I certainly did not indicate that a person as responsible as I am well known to be did not in fact have access to a river.

Another, and surely the best, reason to work with a designer is that you eliminate your husband, who never did want to play any part in the great upheaval. Also, a designer will not answer a question by asking a question. If you ask him whether or not this chair will look good in the corner he may say, "It's a beautiful chair but it's rather too fragile for the sofa and that color will not ride on the carpet." All right, you've learned something.

Well, everything is all assembled now and looks dandy, but not so dandy that the boys are required to remove their shoes before entering—a custom that is, I am told, widespread in Japan.

Much as I would like to, something I can't promise is that if you redecorate your house and work with an interior designer you will lose twenty pounds. But the fact of the matter is, I did.

The Larchmont, New York home of Jean and Walter
Kerr and their six children rests on a point of land
overlooking Long Island Sound. A rambling,
fifteen-room Tudor-style residence, it was originally
the coach house and stables of an estate. Charles B.
King, an early partner of Henry Ford, subsequently
purchased the property and restored it.

OPPOSITE: *A stone lion, purchased by the Kerrs in
Venice, guards the entrance doors, which came from a
demolished New Rochelle church.*

RIGHT: *The view from a balcony above the Living
Room takes in a late-Gothic-style chimneypiece
adorned with a series of clown figures by Martini.
The floor came from the old Sloane mansion in New
York City.* Jean Kerr, author and playwright (**Mary,
Mary; Please Don't Eat the Daisies** and many
others) recalls: "After years of benign neglect our
house was beginning to look like one of those small,
off-season resort hotels that cater to transient
students." Deciding that redecoration was necessary,
she enlisted the aid of New York interior designer
F. Wayne Stellmacher.

167

The commodious 25-by-35-foot Living Room has 14-foot
ceilings and tall leaded-glass windows with small insets of
painted figures and bottle glass. The view through the large bay
window includes the movement of pleasure craft on the Sound.
Warm deep-toned paneling on walls and ceiling are from the
William K. Vanderbilt house in New York City. Armless side
chairs create a conversation setting with sofa and club chair.
Antique silver candelabrum and lamps were purchased by Jean
Kerr's mother at antiques shops in Ireland. The ceramic figure
on horseback atop the piano is a memento of a trip to Venice.

Soft-toned upholstery fabrics in the Living Room, including crewel, velvet and suede cloth, coordinate with a custom-made rug. Mrs. Kerr found her visits to fabric houses with Wayne Stellmacher somewhat disconcerting: "It's fortunate that you have a designer with you, because, if you're like me, you tend to come unglued in the presence of such a prodigality of choices, and can do nothing but hum Gershwin songs under your breath."

LEFT: *Posters, photographs and books crowd the walls of critic and author Walter Kerr's 20-by-30-foot Study, a highly personalized workroom. When Broadway's Martinique Theater underwent remodeling, the Kerrs purchased some of its original seats—apropos memorabilia for the dean of New York's drama critics and a specialist in drama theory.*
BELOW LEFT: *An Italian painted commode stands beneath a gilded Baroque mirror in the paneled Dining Room. The candelabra are nineteenth-century French bronze, with porcelain inserts.*
OPPOSITE: *Candlelight and a bronze-and-crystal chandelier illuminate the 20-by-20-foot Dining Room's soft light tones. Much animated conversation takes place at the onyx-topped dining table, which is supported by three gilded dolphins. The velvet-upholstered chairs, with an interesting English-inspired design, are painted and gilded. The Kerrs purchased most of the furnishings for this room in Italy, including the tall painted cabinet containing rare china and other collectables. They were looking for a very shallow piece to fit this particular space, so the Italian dealer—confused a bit by language problems—sold them his own display case. Such adventures in living come naturally to the Kerrs, whose unique and entertaining personalities are reflected in their comfortable, congenial home.*

LEE RADZIWILL

After eighteen years of living in a Belgravia house renowned for the sumptuousness of its Oriental décor, and in a country place that was "a bower of flowers," Lee Radziwill returned to a city she has always loved. Her New York apartment, in a building on the quieter reaches of upper Fifth Avenue, is now the special universe of the multitalented and attractive woman-about-the-world. Into it she has brought the best of both environments she had cherished in England.

Lee Radziwill's strong convictions and to-the-point declarations belie the fragile look and soft voice. "I always begin a room with the rug; it is literally the foundation of the space. I then go on to the furniture. Virtually everything you see here was acquired in London: the Louis XVI chairs, which, incidentally, are by Jacob, the candelabra over the fireplace, and the small English Regency desk." She points to two small oils. "They're Turkish and a necessary part of the Eastern quotations I bring to every room. If I really can be said to have a personal style, I think it is reflected in my taste for the exotic and the unexpected. I like to create rooms that are essentially traditional—and then add touches of the bizarre and the delicious.

"You see," she continues, "my design philosophy is essentially European. I abhor the American idea of getting rid of everything and starting with a tabula rasa every few years. When I buy something, I do so with the intention of keeping it forever. I'm constantly falling in love with objects, and they follow me around the world.

"When I saw this space for the first time," she says of the living room, which spans the width of the apartment, "it was one long room. I immediately decided to make my first and only structural change. I divided the space into two rooms of equal size, both absolutely square. I realized that I would be able to have a much greater degree of flexibility by working within a perfectly classical framework. I've always believed in classic, neutral proportions; they make it possible to create almost any spatial effect you wish."

Suffused with an almost Victorian flush of color, a mélange of warm reds and translucent pinks, the room is cooled with a current of green. Lettuce-colored draperies are at the windows, and flashes of verdure pass from the paintings to the large Korean vase that stands in one corner and the massed orchids that float in another.

"The nineteenth century is my period," confides Lee Radziwill. "Of course that gives me a wide canvas to work with. I adore the fine Empire and Regency work of the earlier decades, but I also have an affinity for the more elaborate aesthetic of the Victorians. Their sense of decorative freedom, their enthusiasm for exotica and for

collecting amuses me."

A gaze around the room encompasses a fifth-century Roman head, a French Rococo mirror, and the stylized garden of a Bessarabian rug underfoot. Here is an unusual ability at work, a synthesizing taste that joins times and cultures in total harmony.

The hall is an important visual component of the overall scheme of the apartment. A superb Francis Bacon is hung on gray-blue velvet. It is a magisterial work, dominating the room with its tensely resolved composition, quivering with the energy and fury of the twentieth century. The dialogue between the living room and the hall links two epochs, brought to a resolution by resonating greens and reds.

The dining room continues the axis of the living room and hall, restating several themes of the apartment. A moiré fabric covers the walls and is matched by curtains. Here the "Oriental quotations" are nineteenth-century Indian glass paintings. The dining table and chairs are outstanding Regency pieces, their tawny surfaces a continuation of the speckled textures that appear everywhere, as in the intriguing tortoiseshell card case collection on a Library table.

The upper floor of the apartment is totally opposed in mood to the living areas, but the underlying principles are the same. The concern for the richness and ambiguity of surface color appears again in the bedroom. The frames of a fine collection of nineteenth-century botanical watercolors are painted in trompe l'oeil, to simulate marble, while the bedroom furniture, which consists of pieces from several periods, is united by painted surfaces. This gives the room a guileless country air, a pleasing counterpoint to the more sophisticated qualities that prevail in the living room.

"I like to imagine I'm in the country when I'm up here," explains Lee Radziwill, and certainly the leafy extremities of Central Park, glimpsed through the windows, enhance the illusion of rural living.

"I think that the two things I have tried to deal with in creating my own home are intangible: light and life. The former is so important to me. I love the sun and the sky, the movement of light. I composed all the rooms to reflect that sense. Life, of course, comes from the plants that I absolutely surround myself with. Green flowers fascinate me: lilies, bells-of-Ireland, and a marvelous zinnia called 'Envy.'

"What I believe in most of all is simplicity. Lovely things look best when displayed against clear, honest backgrounds. I've never cared for the pattern-on-pattern school. I think a home should be a very calm oasis in this hectic world of ours."

173

The Living Room of Lee Radziwill's Fifth Avenue apartment is suffused with Victorian warmth and effectively placed touches of the exotic.

OPPOSITE: *A blazing fire in the marble fireplace brightens the already vibrant colors. A serene fifth-century Roman head rests on the mantel. Buillotte lamps on the Louis XVI tables flanking the fireplace illuminate portraits of a Turkish noble and his lady. Nineteenth-century English paintings by James Ward chronicle a boar-hunting expedition in India. The pair of gilded creme Louis XVI chairs were designed by Georges Jacob.*

RIGHT: *The Victorian/Oriental/Louis XVI mixture is continued into another portion of the room. A third Ward painting extends the boar hunt group to a space above a Louis XVI clock on a demilune commode, while twin tusks project their spiraled elegance on either side of the commode.*

BELOW RIGHT: *A Bessarabian rug provides a stylized garden on which to rest much of Lee Radziwill's exotic European and Eastern treasures, though a dromedary figure in repose on a lacquered table seems blissfully unaware of its stylish surroundings.*

175

ABOVE: *One corner of the Living Room is a miniaturization of the décor. An antique inkstand rests on the small Sheraton writing desk. Nearby is a Louis XVI footstool. A nineteenth-century painting introduces a sensuous note.*
OPPOSITE: *Picturesque carved dolphins form the pedestal of a Regency Dining Room table ornamented with a lily-bedecked silver épergne. Delicate Regency chairs, with hocked legs and fragile arms and backs, have seat cushions of tiger-striped velvet. Against the wall a Regency chest with bamboo posts is accented by a Greek key motif. Above it a natty monkey and his canine friend, in an eighteenth-century English painting by John Wootton, inject a note of frivolity. Moiré wall upholstery intensifies the period warmth.*

Tôle paintings of the four continents preside benignly over the aureate tones of the Library. "I adore the fine Empire and Regency work of earlier decades," says Lee Radziwill, "but I also have an affinity for the more elaborate aesthetic of the Victorians." Generously adapted French fabrics cover walls, windows, upholstered pieces and Regency benches. Stenciling on the wall drapery fabric creates an architectural element. A bronze lion stalks an invisible prey across the low table, while a collection of tortoiseshell card cases on the table at left adds a warm personal touch. At the right, the Oriental theme is provided by an Indian genre panel between paintings representing Africa and Asia.

Nineteenth-century hand-tinted botanical prints and a floral chintz fabric give the Master Bedroom a light, airy mien. The painted Venetian table and English canopy bed add informal elegance. A Sheraton wheel-back chair and a French voyeuse contribute to the period charm.

LEFT: *The floral motif of the Master Bedroom extends to a nineteenth-century glass découpage lamp, which in turn illuminates another pair of botanical watercolors. A cherished portrait of the late President Kennedy with daughter Caroline stands next to a solitary flower.*

BELOW LEFT: *Prints of flowers and fruit are also focal points of daughter Tina's Bedroom, with the vibrant tones of the walls and curtain fabric adding their lushness. An antique Portuguese porcelain-and-brass bed reiterates the Victorian theme. Both bedrooms reflect one of Lee Radziwill's personal design philosophies: "Lovely things look best when displayed against clear, honest backgrounds."*

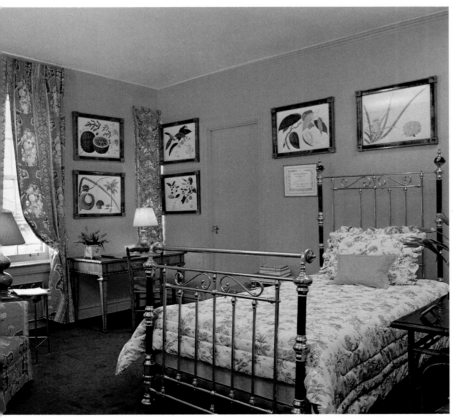

DIANA VREELAND

There are no two ways about it. Diana Vreeland is a rare contemporary "character": a human find, rewarding for being both unique and authentic.

Born in Paris, the daughter of a Scottish father and an American mother, she was brought up in a privileged, between-the-wars European world. Happily married, to T. Reed Vreeland, and the devoted mother of two sons, she might easily have subsided with grace into a conventional life. Instead, after the Vreelands settled permanently in New York City, in 1937, she began a career in international fashion—twenty-five years as fashion editor of *Harper's Bazaar*, followed by a provocative reign as editor-in-chief of *Vogue.*

The trajectory of influence continues to widen and deepen. Since 1971 she has served as special consultant to the Costume Institute of the Metropolitan Museum of Art, solidifying her original and extraordinary contribution to the history of taste.

Her residence is nearly as much an establishment as its occupant. "Anyone who can photograph this place would find the Sistine chapel a cinch," Diana Vreeland says with a wry smile.

The wit is legendary, and as essential a part of Mrs. Vreeland's personality as her addiction to an oddly poetic oral shorthand. Her spontaneous remarks—"Pink is the navy blue of India," and "I want my apartment to look like a garden: a garden in hell!"—have been reiterated into a litany by her admirers. However, her apartment, while it accords well enough with expectations of the unusual, is certainly not "a garden in hell," despite the undeniable abundance of the color *red*—red carpets, red-lacquered doors, red closet linings and picture frames. And, aside from the flamboyant scarlet-flowered cotton of the wallcoverings and draperies of the living room, it is not particularly horticultural.

As New York apartments go, it is modest in size, principally composed of an entrance hall, an *L*-shaped living room and two bedrooms.

Despite its relatively limited space, the living room area has been used to full advantage. Its focal point is a capacious sofa with an impressive rampart of cushions. The not especially distinguished proportions of the room are deftly disguised by screens and mirrors.

Designer Billy Baldwin, who helped with the interiors, is one of Mrs. Vreeland's oldest and closest friends. The prevailing feeling he achieves is one of warmth and smoothness, comfort and privacy. The ambience is so subtly, unemphatically strong and pervasive that the existence of the teeming city beyond the windows is only casually or sporadically sensed.

Mrs. Vreeland's bedroom, lined and curtained with a blue-grounded Spanish-made version of the scarlet-flowered cotton print of the living room, has something of the same quality.

There is nothing to indicate that she habitually works at home in the mornings; there is a very pretty red-lacquered Chinese desk not far from the bed, but, like her dressing table, it is all but submerged in personal memorabilia. Her office area consists of a few square feet of space in her bathroom, close to a telephone.

It is easy to absorb to the full the visible charm of the apartment, but the inner significance can be conveyed only by Diana Vreeland herself. Nearly every object is intimately connected with the owner's life story.

Books are everywhere, an enviably idiosyncratic selection. The wall-length bookcase in the dining area includes many seventeenth- and twentieth-century French classics, plus a favorite shelf Mrs. Vreeland calls "my Oriental department."

She says, "I could live *only* with books." But actually, the bookcases in both parts of the living room serve also to hold a part of the heterogeneous horde of personal possessions: *objets trouvés,* collections, drawings, paintings and photographs. The collections—Scottish horns, seashells, Staffordshire dogs, Battersea enamel—consist almost in their entirety of gifts from friends. The objects—"mostly just things of no value that I picked up on travels"—also include a notable present or two: an exquisite little crown, for instance, once worn by the ballerina Karsavina.

Among the paintings and drawings are pencil portraits by Jean Oberlé of Reed Vreeland and the Vreeland sons, and an oil painting of their elder son by Nora Auric, "a surprise birthday present." In the foyer hangs a beguiling portrait of Diana Vreeland painted by William Acton in Florence in 1934. On the wall of the dining area of the living room is an equally enchanting portrait of her in a turban, painted by Ned Murray. Nearby hangs Augustus John's pencil portrait, accompanied by a galaxy of sketches of her by two of her dearest friends, Cecil Beaton and the late Christian Bérard.

There is an abundance of photographs of family and old friends, including the Duke of Windsor in a kilt, which he had donned at Diana Vreeland's insistence and with the encouragement of the duchess; photographs of colleagues Carmel Snow, Marie-Louise Bousquet, Margaret Case. The whole array is a touching testimony to the Vreeland genius for friendship.

However, it is Diana Vreeland herself who emerges as the star of the mise-en-scène, precisely because it is so truthful a reflection of her private self—dynamic, picturesque, an authentic force in the world of style.

Diana Vreeland's remarkable life as an important force in the world of fashion and taste is quite literally in evidence throughout her New York apartment. Photographs and personal memorabilia are everywhere, in a setting of richly colored fabrics that create a swirl of textures and patterns. With wry perspicacity she observes, "Anyone who could photograph this place would find the Sistine chapel a cinch."
RIGHT: *On one side of the Living Room peonies spill over a writing table laden with personal treasures. The hand and the cat in the photograph at the right are those of the French writer Colette. Two fashion sketches by Christian Bérard hang near a draped Venetian blackamoor mirror; one of the drawings is of Mrs. Vreeland. The mounted porcelains above the mirror have playing-card designs. In the foreground a bemused china tiger and an imperturbable llama stand guard over the collection.*

184

OPPOSITE: "I want my apartment to look like a garden — a garden in hell!" says Diana Vreeland. The Living Room does suggest a lush garden in which red replaces green, dominated by brilliant Indian cotton tree-of-life fabric bought in London. Needlepoint on the playing-card pillows is the work of Mrs. Vreeland. Her parents acquired the seventeenth-century painted leather screen on their honeymoon, in Europe. "There is an infinity of places to sit — mostly low, all comfortable," comments a frequent visitor to the apartment.

ABOVE: The Dining Area is the horizontal stroke of the L-shaped living room. When she entertains, the legendary editor sometimes has her guests congregate in the larger area, while she wanders off to the cozy dining area for a tête-à-tête with one friend. Seashells fill a carved wooden clam shell attributed to Grinling Gibbons, and others are displayed on blackamoor brackets along the main wall. The V painting by Alexander Liberman, on the left, rests on a wooden angel figure found in the Paris Flea Market. On the right, a blackamoor console table supports a Scottish drinking horn mounted in brass. An antique American bull's-eye mirror reflects treasures in another portion of the room.

ABOVE RIGHT: A tall screen serves to separate the dining area. from the luxuriously draped living room.

OPPOSITE: *In Diana Vreeland's Bedroom, the silk printed scarf
lying on the French blanket cover is where her shoes and
handbag are laid out in the evening. Mrs. Vreeland calls her
bedroom "a very happy room to be in." Wall and curtain
fabric, the same pattern as the one in the living room, but a
different color, was made in Spain.*

ABOVE: *The bed, designed by Syrie Maugham, is reflected in a
Louis XVI mirror. On the table are cowrie shells, Battersea
enameled boxes and family pictures, including a photograph of
Mrs. Vreeland's husband, the late T. Reed Vreeland, in a
red-lacquered frame.*

POLLY BERGEN

Actress, singer, business executive and mother of two, Polly Bergen's commitments are legion. A part-time resident of both coasts, she chose to live in Malibu because it is a very special place that combines glamour with the casual life. "I am a working person," she says. "I cannot function without a nest."

Designer Frank Austin had been designing interiors for Miss Bergen for over a decade when she called on him for her new home at the beach. He comments, "She's secure enough to always use a designer. Many women *think* they have great taste, but Polly really does. She has a great flair for making the best out of any situation.

"Her sense of proportion is superb. When she does a house, she looks at the space, at all the possibilities, decides how it would work, and should work. She knows exactly what she wants and has the rare ability to follow through. This was the first house that she really did on her own, and she knew that she wanted it to be a 'Polly Bergen interior.' "

"I couldn't have done all this without Frank," Miss Bergen admits without hesitation. "But I didn't want any particular designer's look."

"She gave me ideas by talking of places she'd been, or something she had seen, to convey how she was feeling and how she wanted to live at that time," Mr. Austin explains. "Polly doesn't decorate for posterity. She decorates for the present and the immediate future."

The two discussed placement extensively, in the planning stage. Mr. Austin continues, "Polly didn't want to bring twenty things in when ten would do. She doesn't force into a house what can't happen." Miss Bergen selected pieces from her former house, everything she felt was part of her, but only what would fit in with her new mode of living.

Mr. Austin modified antiques when necessary. "Good things always work. Why buy a new table to fill up a space? We cut a North African oval table down to sofa height," he recounts. "It's the perfect size and can take care of eight for dinner, in the informal way she likes to do most of her entertaining.

"Above all, we strove for flexibility. She wanted the house to be very, very light, and also very dramatic. It was to be casual, yet stylish. It had to encompass and move in all these directions."

Because they felt that an all-white look wasn't right for the beach, they decided to work from the colors of Malibu—the browns of the hills and the gray and beige of the sand, with a touch of Pacific blue. "We painted the beams dark, for a dramatic effect, and put a pickled-wash finish on the ceiling to reflect the sand. The floors are bleached and weathered to blend with the terrain."

By mixing period pieces with modern, Mr. Austin achieved the right mix of formality and informality. In the dining area a lacquered Persian screen is juxtaposed with a whimsically painted contemporary table. Miss Bergen wanted textured fabric, so Frank Austin chose linen velvet. "Most people think velvet is a dressy fabric," he observes, "but it can be very casual, because it is soft. Linen velvet moves both ways."

Although the house was simplified for practical purposes, the only major structural change was made in the master bedroom, upstairs. This sunny room is, in a most compelling way, exact and strong and assured—like Polly Bergen herself. It was planned to serve a dual function as a refuge and an office.

Like most entertainers, Miss Bergen has an extensive wardrobe, so a long wall was constructed to afford storage space. It was Miss Bergen's idea to have the bath open to the bedroom, for a sense of luxurious ease in her private domain, and the closet wall also acts as a link between the bedroom and bath area. Its doors mirror the ocean view, creating an expanded sense of space. Miss Bergen calls the bedroom her "butterfly room," because the reflection creates a double image, like wings unfolded. The bath is adorned with paintings, art objects and an antique mirror that was a gift from Napoleon to the Empress Josephine.

"For me, comfort is the first requisite," Miss Bergen remarks. "I don't like to live carefully—to watch glass so it won't be broken, to have furniture you can't sit on. This house is far simpler than many others I've had. Formerly the décor was inclined to be more theatrical, more overpowering. But this house is me. It's a place where I can relax, work without interruptions and entertain easily—something, by the way, I enjoy tremendously."

According to her friends, Polly Bergen is a skilled hostess, capable of masterminding a large party and making each guest feel the center of attention. She and Mr. Austin carefully planned the seating and lighting arrangements of the living and dining areas to accommodate intimate groupings. There are few floor lamps; instead, a grid of surface-mounted lights on the ceiling illuminates each area individually so that a foursome playing cards in one corner need not intrude on a group conversing by candlelight elsewhere.

Miss Bergen often puts large pillows and cushions on the floor and her guests sit around the low North African table, sharing good food and talk.

Her house at Malibu is a way of life that perfectly suits her personal style. If her life changes, she will change her environment. She adds thoughtfully, "I learned late in life who I am. Now I'll never lose perspective on myself."

Polly Bergen recognizes that she needs a "nest," to function in her demanding roles as actress, singer and busy executive. She and designer Frank Austin continued a working association of nearly fifteen years in creating a "Polly Bergen interior" for her Malibu beach residence.

OPPOSITE: *Cool and serene, the Living Room is exotically appointed with a Louis XVI gilt mirror, and a custom-designed opium bed, laden with pillows. A low North African table with a glass center and intricate filigree work serves as a dining table for informal entertaining; guests often sit casually on cushions surrounding the table. Instead of lamps, surface-mounted ceiling lights illuminate various areas of the room, allowing small groups to function independently and with a mood of intimacy. Beyond a wall of sliding glass doors is a terrace and the vast stretch of the Pacific Ocean.*

ABOVE: *The Dining Area reveals rich hardwood floors to their full advantage. Pieces from Miss Bergen's Steuben crystal collection adorn the custom-painted contemporary table. A Persian screen details one corner of the room while an Early American carved wood horse above the fireplace adds a folk art touch to the well-planned scene. Painting by Faris.*

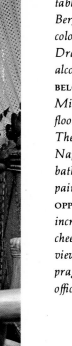

LEFT: *An Emmy, won for the title role in* The Helen Morgan Story, *stands prominently on a glass-topped table in the Guest Room, where awards marking Polly Bergen's career cover a wall. Muted tones, spiced with colorful pillow accents, help create a restful atmosphere. Drapery treatment divides the space into a sleeping alcove and sitting area.*

BELOW LEFT: *The Master Bath is incorporated into Miss Bergen's commodious bedroom, on the second floor, offering an airy feeling of comfort and luxury. The antique mirror was originally a gift from Napoleon Bonaparte to Josephine. Wide tub ledges hold bath accoutrements and Chinese pottery figures. The painted ceiling fan adds a lighthearted touch.*

OPPOSITE: *Mirrored doors concealing a large wardrobe increase the spaciousness of Polly Bergen's bright and cheerful Bedroom while restating the exhilarating ocean view and a painting by Sardi. The décor is clean and pragmatic—a feminine environment that serves as both office and refuge for a vital personality.*

TRUMAN CAPOTE

It is virtually impossible to find his Long Island home in the Hamptons—and that's exactly the way Truman Capote wants it. His two-story house of weathered shingles is hidden behind scrub pine, privet hedges and rows of hydrangea bushes.

The celebrated author lives near Sagaponack, on the South Fork, in the heart of the Hamptons—a stretch of rolling potato fields and lush farmlands shouldering the nearby Atlantic Ocean. It is a year-round farming community and a summer place for city people, where antique farmhouses vie with modernistic glass houses for the dunes and fields. Mr. Capote once called Sagaponack "Kansas with a sea breeze."

The best way to find the rather secluded house is to be with Mr. Capote as he sits at the wheel of his deep-green Buick. It is a short but bumpy ride down a dirt lane, first opened in 1670, a quick turn into a gravel driveway, which passes a natural bird sanctuary and a friend's cottage built on the author's property, before he pulls up in front of his box-shaped, flat-roofed wooden house.

"I own these fields," he says, proudly sweeping his left hand toward the six acres he acquired in 1962, when he had the house built.

"It was done by a local carpenter, who's dead now. It's exactly the way I wanted it. I work at this untended look; it's intentional. You can tell how quiet it is here, because you can barely see the top of another house. This is a place to be alone.

"I'm not out here to entertain," explains Mr. Capote. "I'm here to work. I come here a lot in the autumn and winter, and I see almost no one. I don't care for the Hamptons as much in the summer—too crowded.

"I spend most of my time here reading, writing, going for walks with my dog and talking on the telephone. In New York I see people; but I don't see New York people out here." At Sagaponack there is company enough, with Maggie, his celebrated English bulldog.

"In all the years I've had this house, I've gone out six times for dinner. Now that's quite a record, for someone known for being so social, isn't it?"

Entering his house through the back kitchen door, he removes his loafers and walks into the living room. There the barefoot Mr. Capote picks up a rag mop as delicately as Fred Astaire might tap his dancing cane, and starts to dust the marine-blue floor, still not quite dry from its recent coat of deck paint.

"I've just had it repainted," he says, "and this humidity doesn't help it dry. You should see the room at night. The floor floats like a big blue-green lake."

The author describes his house as a "raincoat," referring to the method of its construction. Built with the exterior walls exposed inside to reveal vertical studs and horizontal bracings, the "skin" of the building protects the interior, in many ways like a raincoat.

"I wanted a rustic house. I really think of it as one big room. Completely winterized, it's been designed to look unfinished. I call it 'run-down comfort.' "

A large floor-to-ceiling window with divided panes lets in the glorious morning sun and allows a view of the sea and sand some two hundred yards beyond the house. A spiraling steel staircase leads to a balconied second floor study. Here he works or reads.

He designs his own interiors. "For me, it's a bore to use a decorator. I don't care about having someone come in and tell me what I need. I *know*."

His philosophy of good interior design? "Something that's not immediately offensive when you walk in. Of course it may be, eventually."

All of his furniture is comfortable, attractive, to be used rather than looked at. A priceless Tiffany lamp illuminates the shoulder of a worn yellow-velvet easy chair; upholstery has a few sun-faded patches; clusters of glass paperweights glisten. Some of the wicker tables and chairs are from inexpensive import shops; others, including the sturdy table where Mr. Capote writes, are from antiques stores.

Off the enormous living room is a small screened-in porch, similar to those found in many Southern homes. Mr. Capote uses it as a summer room when the breezes blow mildly from the sea. His bedroom, near the kitchen, is stark and sparsely furnished.

"I like to have my own things around me," observes Mr. Capote, whose permanent base is a sleek apartment in the U.N. Plaza in Manhattan. "Even when I travel to my other houses, in Switzerland and California, I take things of my own with me."

A picture taken several years ago by society photographer Slim Aarons shows a youthful Capote perched on a Victorian sofa, surrounded by favorite objects. "I like to collect things, Victorian things, and mix everything together. I enjoy looking for and at all of them. I'm not sure I need them. I've got too much and I haven't edited myself with care lately!"

Truman Capote's *Breakfast at Tiffany's* begins with the line, "I am always drawn back to places where I have lived, the houses and the neighborhoods."

"I moved around so much as a child," he remarks, "I never had a sense of home. Maybe I did when I was eleven and lived in a rural town in Alabama." Eyeing a hat rack above his brick fireplace, the writer points to his assortment of rumpled Panamas, and laughs. "Home is where I hang my hats."

The two-story Living Room of author Truman Capote's Long Island home, in the Hamptons, projects the aura of oceanside seclusion preferred by its owner.

LEFT: An overview of the room points up Mr. Capote's whimsical nature. At the far left a pottery French bulldog stares questioningly at the viewer, while a sanguine lion contemplates a quartet of glass paperweights. The gorilla vase to the right of the wine rack seems to be showing off a floral headdress, and a horn chair covered in tiger-striped fabric interjects a slightly Eastern influence. The red-lacquered low table supports calico and porcelain cats, a pair of land-loving fish and a miniature donkey, driver and cart.

ABOVE: On the stepped "witchcraft altar," the mask designed by Jean Cocteau, on a needlepoint pillow, is reminiscent of the central character in the poet's film **La Belle et la Bête**. A bronze nineteenth-century weight rests solidly behind an antique American wooden toy cat.

OPPOSITE: The fireplace hearth and mantel, like the rest of the room, has become a repository for a mélange of favored items. A formidable sculpted boar regards an equally determined needlepoint bulldog. A hatrack above brings to mind Mr. Capote's famous assortment of Panama hats. "I keep leaving them when I go to visit people," he remarks. "I don't have as many as I used to because I don't recover them all. People always promise to send them back to me, but they don't."

RIGHT: *A small corner of Mr. Capote's Living Room sparkles modestly as the light from a jewel-toned Tiffany lamp dances through the facets and patterns of a collection of glass paperweights. A nineteenth-century botanical study contrasts with framed personal photographs, while a fluid Art Nouveau butterfly alights amid the sturdy geometrics of the paperweights, counterpointing its owner's chimerical nature.*

BELOW: *The aquatic tones of the furniture, floor, lampshades and tinted lenses of Mr. Capote's glasses intensify the seaside atmosphere of the cottage. Here the author works on new projects and indulges his English bulldog, Maggie, who occasionally ventures abroad to raid unsuspecting picnickers' baskets on nearby Gibson beach.*

RIGHT: *Mr. Capote's temperate Bedroom is a continuation of the sparse motif seen throughout the house. His cot-sized English brass bed is usually flanked by stacks of detective magazines and books. An antique mirror and miniature chests of drawers are niched between the exposed studs, formalizing, yet at the same time warming, the quarters.*

BELOW RIGHT: *The weathered exterior of the studio/beach house amplifies the pervasive feeling of seclusion. Secreted deep in the lush farmlands of the Hamptons, the residence was built to the author's specifications, in 1962, by a local carpenter who successfully captured the intentional "untended look." "You can tell how quiet it is here, because you can barely see the top of another house," says Mr. Capote. "This is a place to be alone." The international celebrity's solitude is interrupted only occasionally by invited house guests from throughout the world, as well as by neighboring friends such as Joseph Heller, James Jones, Willem de Kooning and Jean Stafford.*

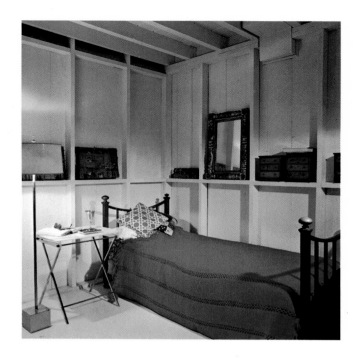

Shelving containing some of the author's favorite books and memorabilia extends from the living room to the Loft. Treetops glimpsed from second story windows assume a dreamlike quality as mists from the nearby Atlantic soften and partially obscure their verdant tones. Other paperweights and small decorated boxes may be glimpsed just beneath the balcony, while the ever-present curvilinear lines of wicker furniture appoint the area. A colorful pillow garden rests atop the sofa, creating an indoor feeling of spring. The drawing in the center of the loft bookshelves is a pencil portrait of Mr. Capote by René Bouché.

JOAN CRAWFORD

Her career as an actress spanned much of American film history, and she was equally successful in a second career as a businesswoman.

"I live today in order to plan for tomorrow," the late Joan Crawford philosophized. Her functional environment reflected her varied activities, and the work desk alone told a story of formidable organization. Although her Manhattan apartment was a crisp and compact home, belying the myth that at least a dozen rooms are necessary to live like a star, it demonstrated the enviable élan of her previous residences.

Hollywood has long favored the Manhattan skyline as a backdrop for its great dramas. A tableau of streamlined towers seen through a high-rise window seems a perfect setting for a legendary star.

Film actor turned interior designer, the late William Haines was Miss Crawford's decorator for her first home in Hollywood and worked with her through the years until they reached the apotheosis of East Seventieth Street in Manhattan, the multiroom duplex where she spent happy years as Mrs. Alfred E. Steele.

Her association with Mr. Haines dated back to her early days at Metro-Goldwyn-Mayer. "I was practically raised by Billy Haines," she said. "He was like a big brother to me. He would show me the differences between Hepplewhite and Chippendale. I'd look things up, read, and soon I reached the point where I was able to talk to him in his own language.

"All my taste is acquired," she used to say. "As I was exposed to various periods and styles, I learned, and as I learned, I adapted—a color, an idea." The artistic direction came from Mr. Haines. He designed many pieces of furniture for the Seventieth Street apartment, in a mode that might be termed California Modern. It is a style that has already acquired period identification.

"Then when I moved to this apartment," Miss Crawford related, "designer Carleton Varney and I worked with many of Billy's pieces. I just couldn't give up all the things he had done. I told Carleton to bear in mind that I didn't want anything elegant. I wanted something to really function for me."

The logic of the apartment was confirmed in the gleaming well-equipped kitchen, which reminded Miss Crawford of a William Haines maxim that she fondly repeated: " 'If the kitchen is in the right spot, everything else will fall into place.' I love cooking," she added, "so to me the kitchen is as important as the dining room. Home is a place to welcome friends, make them comfortable and give them delicious things to eat."

She liked a certain background for her guests, her pictures and her plants. In each Manhattan apartment she introduced a cheerful California feeling, with pure white walls and bright colors. She kept the rooms filled with flowers and plants.

Carleton Varney worked with Joan Crawford for ten years. "Joan was a terribly generous person," he remarks. "She never failed to send a thank you note, or call when you were ill. Everything about her was very precise, and this was reflected in the way we worked together. For instance, when we laid out a room, she had masking tape put down on the floor. She liked to walk around it and sense the way a room was going to work. Joan was used to this from the studio sets, where she would have to rehearse before the furniture arrived."

Mr. Varney was able to incorporate such diverse Haines pieces as the living room sofa and an agate marble coffee table of unique design, and to mix in contemporary classics like the yellow Parsons dining table. In the living room, green and white fabric features a Chinese-character motif. "He told me it means 'I love you, Joan,' " Miss Crawford would say with her famous smile.

"I believe that a client gives a designer three things," Carleton Varney comments. "First, time. Joan was marvelous when it came to waiting for things to arrive. Second, budget. Well, the budget here was for using things that Joan already had, and tailoring them to the new environment. Three, taste. Or as I prefer to call it, experience. In this case it involved not just her own experience, but that of another designer as well. And you must remember that a person like Joan Crawford had obviously collected a vast quantity of objects over the years, to say nothing of the myriad of personal things. As far as the apartment is concerned, let's say that I was more a cosmetician than anything else. I changed the dress of the furniture, rather than the pieces themselves. By deepening the lighter-toned pieces to a darker, teak hue, I was able to accentuate her collection of white Kuan-yin porcelains. By setting everything against white and green, we achieved a clean functional look."

Typically, Miss Crawford wanted a cold honest light for her dressing table. A star does not remain a star by being sentimental, but by dealing with the facts.

Did Miss Crawford have any regrets about leaving California for a more compact New York life? "No," was the answer. "I remember the glorious parties in my garden, but I never think of who owns my house now. I really enjoy looking forward, not back."

Joan Crawford lived with her eyes turned toward the future. "All my nostalgia is for tomorrow—not for any yesterdays," she said resolutely. "I have the same sense of excitement about the next adventure in life as I had when I was sixteen."

RIGHT: *A bronze bust by Salamunich conveys the strength and optimism of Joan Crawford, whose glamour graced motion picture screens for decades. In recent years she had also developed a successful second career, in the business world, and it was a determining factor in her highly organized way of life. When Miss Crawford moved to a new Manhattan apartment, more compact than her former duplex, she told interior designer Carleton Varney that she didn't want anything elegant: "I want something to really function for me."*

BELOW: *The crisp Living Room shows the influence of the late William Haines, who for years designed interiors for Miss Crawford. Pieces of furniture he created for her have acquired a period quality; Mr. Varney retained and freshened them with bright fabric accents. He also darkened the woods to a teak shade. The atmosphere is cool, clear and light: "I can't stand dark walls," Miss Crawford declared. "I want pure, unadulterated pristine white. That's the kind of background I like for my guests, my pictures and my plants."*

OPPOSITE: *The face of Joan Crawford, a study in contrast by Michaele Vollbracht, illustrates her star quality.*

OPPOSITE: *A Parsons table in the Living Room functions as a desk, in what was essentially a working environment. It also serves as a recognition of change; Joan Crawford updated her environment—just as she always adjusted her screen portrayals—to keep pace with contemporary taste. The paraphernalia of a busy and carefully planned professional life remain in view, close at hand. Spatial divisions in the simplified design permit separate areas to function independently, yet the total room remains unified by color.*

OPPOSITE BELOW: *Oriental porcelains and other collectables fill a colorful niche in the Dining Area, while comfortable floor pillows reiterate the color scheme. The custom-built dining table was used alternately as an additional work surface. Varney-designed fabric for the screen and draperies includes a Chinese-character motif: "He told me it means 'I love you, Joan,'" Miss Crawford used to say, smiling.*

LEFT: *Typically unsparing white light—the kind used for applying theatrical makeup—illuminates Joan Crawford's custom-designed dressing table. Designer Varney created the subtly patterned monochromatic draperies that define the Dressing Area. Other clues to the Academy Award-winning star's interests—Oriental figurines and a grouping of books—rest on a tea cart nearby; many more books and porcelains are displayed on numerous shelves in other areas of the apartment.*

BELOW LEFT: *A soft-toned fabric with a geometrically conceived floral motif covers the headboard and bed, and drapes the windows in Miss Crawford's Bedroom. Custom-designed cantilevered bedside tables provide storage and surface space. Bare polished parquet flooring throughout the apartment augments the sparing tailored décor. The crisp harmonious atmosphere was well suited to the nature of a personality noted for precision and vitality.*

JEAN ARTHUR

The weathered redwood frame house is situated on a low bluff that juts out into the Pacific. *Driftwood,* the home of actress Jean Arthur, is a sanctuary set in Carmel, California, fabled for its natural beauty. The view, with ocean on three sides, is spectacular.

The mornings are often foggy here, just north of Big Sur and south of Monterey, and the wind sweeps clouds of mist from the ocean. They veil the knoll and the twisted cypress trees pushing out from rocks along the drive that leads to Miss Arthur's home. The trees seem to take on human or animal forms, reaching out in the misty blue light or settling like great birds on the rocks.

A redwood gate stands slightly ajar, and two stone rabbits stare curiously from the garden. "Come in, come in," they seem to be saying.

This is the private world that reveals Miss Arthur's sensitivity and subtle sense of humor. The space is generous, the atmosphere somewhat austere, and there is a deep feeling of serenity, broken only by the wind song of the cypresses and the distant roar of the ocean.

The mist rises, and in clear patches various images are revealed: a bronze Pan playing his flute in a rectangular garden niche; the bronze head of a goat, on a stone plinth, looking wise and saucy as goats sometimes do; pewter penguins standing among pots of flowering begonias; a crane sheltered by a bonsai red maple; and finally, a glorious striped yellow cat—real—standing watch.

Miss Arthur is at the door, an energetic elf still, her blue eyes sparkling and her hair in Dutch-boy bangs. In that famous husky voice that crackles and slides, she addresses the cat. "The man has come to photograph our house. What do you think of that, Philippe?"

Philippe makes no reply, but trots into the house with his tail straight up. Two more yellow cats are introduced. Fagin, explains Miss Arthur, is from Vassar, and Skipper from North Carolina, where the actress taught theater to college students. There is a fourth cat, Sam, but he hasn't been seen for days. Miss Arthur is worried. Her love and compassion for animals are legendary. She has come to know and understand them.

Once she wanted to keep a lion. "When they are looking at you with those huge eyes you're wondering if they're going to eat you," she once said. "Actually they're wondering if you're going to love them and be good to them." She used to feed the seagulls stew and oatmeal, until the neighbors complained.

Although the locale makes the house seem remote and mysterious, it is never melancholy, for it reflects Jean Arthur's spontaneous gaiety and her love for birds and animals—for everything in nature.

Made of redwood and stone, the house was built in 1908, "on the basis of a sketch drawn one afternoon on brown paper, by a woman who came down from San Francisco," Miss Arthur recounts. "She used it for a summer cottage. It's set on nearly an acre. I rented it, first, then bought it after World War II."

Miss Arthur created the garden with landscape architect George Hoy, who has since retired and lives abroad. Now she cares for it herself with affection and expertise.

The residence is actually two buildings, main house and guest cottage, connected by a twenty-foot walk. In the years since Miss Arthur took up residence there, the interiors have been redecorated a number of times but the general theme, at least in recent years, has been predominantly Oriental.

"I love Japanese architecture for its purity and simplicity," she says. "I wanted to incorporate some of it into the house and garden. You know, this house has a way of telling you what to do. It talks to me, and I listen. For example, the Kwan-on garden room was built as an exercise room and as a place where household plants could go for a rest. Ferns love it out there."

Miss Arthur's response to the life and beauty around her takes a metaphysical form. "How does a pine tree know how to be a pine tree?" she asks. "How does a maple learn to be a maple? It's the greatest magic there is. It's what makes everything be alive. Life by the sea is full of vitality. For me, that vitality is expressed in the trees, in the forms and shadows in the garden that look like animal or human forms. You know, when I sit around the fire in the evening with friends, I catch glimpses of faces in the stone and the firewood and the driftwood. It's part of the enchantment of this place."

Indeed, the fireplace itself seems to take the form of an enormous head with gaping mouth—not menacing, but haunting nonetheless, like the paintings in the living room—one of a ghost ship in the fog and another of fishing schooners putting out to sea. The windows frame Andrew Wyeth-like scenes outside: the pearl gray sea in the soft light of day and the coastal mountains of Big Sur rising in the background.

Living here in total harmony with nature, Miss Arthur feels fulfilled. For her the most important thing in life is feeling; feeling, and being able to learn, expand and evolve. "A tree overcomes and endures everything, to be as beautiful as it can. That's what we should do. Become as strong and beautiful as we can."

Jean Arthur continues to evolve. She hopes to direct Shaw's *Saint Joan* one day. The Maid of Orleans and the Irish playwright are her idols. "The fact that I did not marry George Bernard Shaw is the only real disappointment I've ever had," she smiles happily.

Sinuous Monterey cypress trees challenge gravity in a century-old setting of extraordinary natural beauty. The weathered redwood gate, with Japanese bronze dragon latch, opens to reveal a garden inhabited by stone rabbits and other creatures of pewter and bronze. "Life by the sea is full of vitality," Jean Arthur reflects, from the secluded sanctuary of her Carmel, California residence. "For me, that vitality is expressed in the trees, in the forms and shadows in the garden, which often look like animal or human forms." This rugged outcropping of rocky land meets the Pacific on three sides. Permeating the landscape, the inevitable mist forms a design element as fundamental as trees, shrubs and stones.

212

Four rooms open onto the Atrium, with its glass dome so
accommodating to plants. The feather lines of ibis painted on
wood seem to spread with the grain—the unity of nature's
forms expressed in art. So integral a part of the décor, they
almost seem to have nested here of their own accord, perhaps
shuttling sustenance to their young through an obliging skylight.
The rich blue Japanese slate floor, greened by foliage, is accented
by two Victorian settees, whose curving lines complement the
Oriental motif. "I love Japanese architecture for its simplicity
and purity," the actress comments. "I wanted to incorporate
some of it into the house and garden." The design seems to
include the surging ocean, just yards away.

Tortuous driftwood limbs entwined with grapevines cling to the massive grottolike Living Room fireplace of volcanic rock. A fire glows within, exerting a primeval influence over the entire area. ''When I sit around the fire in the evening with friends, I'm always catching glimpses of faces in the stone and the firewood and the driftwood,'' Jean Arthur muses. Two Chinese sculptured ladies seem to glide toward a leafy cove of driftwood and glass. The floral print of the sofa continues the botanical effect, echoed by a flokati rug. In the background, Japanese lanterns and a painting by E. Hunt detail the hauntingly shadowed walls.

LEFT: *From the Porch a rich tableau extends past the uneven slats of weathered redwood fence encircling the grounds, beyond a wind-scourged cypress and a hazy finger of the Pacific to the mounded heights of the Big Sur coast. The alternate roar and sizzle of the tides announce endless arrivals of cargo—booty of driftwood, shells, seaweed lace and the briny inhabitants of warm tide pools, urged on an already abundant land. No intruder here, this human habitation merges organically with its milieu, integrated into the scheme of natural beauty. Its interiors inevitably incorporate sea traits of color, character and decoration.*

ABOVE: *In the Living Room, carved French mermaid sconces with Irish crystals enhance the oceanic scene in* The Phantom Ship, *by William Ritchel. The Chinese leather chest, crowned by a painted pewter shell, provides a dash of bright color to complement the predominantly subtle tones of the room, a device used throughout the design.*

RIGHT: *Chinese and Japanese features permeate the structure, landscaping and interior décor of the residence, but a vine-covered vitrine reveals in concentrated form Miss Arthur's taste for Far Eastern flavor. Here a jocund Buddha is surrounded by a collection of ornamental Japanese rice bowls, two saucy bisque figurines and a glossy miniature jade plant. Below the cabinet a blackened bronze crab plays beside a top-shaped Japanese bowl.*

The Kwan-on Garden Room was constructed off Miss Arthur's
bedroom, as an exercise area. One end, open to the air and
sunlight, can be closed off by shoji screens, while the rest of the
space is covered by a translucent roof, which allows sunlight to
penetrate in the daytime. Ferns and other plants in need of a
change of environment thrive here.

Kwan-on, goddess of mercy, graces the peaceful court,
mirrored in a reflecting pool of polished wood. A Japanese
candle holder reinforces the meditative atmosphere, while a
French monkey dangling from a rafter creates a comic diversion.
"This house has a way of telling you what to do," Jean Arthur
says. "It talks to me, and I listen."

216

A Japanese stone lantern rises mushroomlike, cap askew,
amidst a congenial miscellany of grass, rocks and attractive
ground covers rumpling the garden floor. The varied plantings,
including spiny aloe and flowering bromeliads, play cameo roles
in obscure nooks, or erect proud stalks on modest promontories.
A small bamboo-topped teahouse finds its reflection in a placid
pond nearby. Aged cypresses, looking like archetypes of trees
meant for climbing and umbrellas blown inside out, form a
loosely woven roof over an airy room without walls. "A tree
overcomes and endures everything, to be as beautiful as it can,"
Jean Arthur reflects. "That's what we should do. Become as
strong and beautiful as we can."

217

JULIA CHILD

It spoke to us the moment we walked in the door. What is now our great gray clapboard Cantabrigian home felt right to us—warm and welcoming—just as our little Georgetown house had felt the moment we walked in, when we lived in Washington between Paul's diplomatic posts. We'd been living abroad off and on since World War II, and we said to ourselves in 1958 that Norway, our next post, would be our last one.

We wanted our permanent residence to be in Cambridge, Massachusetts. If we wanted a house here, said our Cambridge mentor, Avis DeVoto, we'd better start looking around immediately, as good ones were snapped up before they ever hit the open market. She would keep her ears open, she said, and a few weeks before we were to leave for Oslo she called us: "Come immediately."

We arrived in Cambridge promptly at 8:30 A.M., as bidden, and already two other couples were exploring the house. After a good first impression at the front door, we inspected the large cellar, the attic and its adjoining separate apartment, and noted a big room on the second floor that could serve as Paul's studio. On the ground floor we rejoiced in a large airy kitchen with not only one, but two, pantries, a fine dining room and even two living rooms. Our visit took less than twenty minutes, and with no more ado we signed on the dotted line.

Two and a half years later, in the summer of 1961, we returned and took up occupancy. As seems usual with us, we lived in the house during the renovations. Some structural changes were in order, and the interiors needed lightening and brightening. Most of the rooms we left as they were, adding only a stainless-steel sink in the small pantry next to the dining room, with its tall glass-doored cabinets and wide undercabinet drawers. We turned the large pantry into a pastry room, with pegboard walls and a marble-topped work surface. The kitchen, however, needed complete rethinking. We took our problems to architect Robert Woods Kennedy, who is sensitive to old Cambridge houses.

The kitchen proper was our major concern because, to us, it is the beating heart and social center of the household. Although this was our ninth kitchen, we never before had had the luxury of a truly functional, well-proportioned room. We intended to make it both practical and beautiful, a working laboratory as well as a living and dining room. Fortunately all of our structural changes were minor.

Mr. Kennedy suggested we move the double sink from its cramped and original position, crowded against a side wall. Then, since we needed more wall space, he covered up one window with pegboard, for which Paul worked out a stunning arrangement of copper saucepans and skillets. The existing cupboard and drawer arrangements suited us well enough, giving room for our large old restaurant-size gas stove, our wall ovens, chopping block, dishwasher and refrigerator.

Lighting, color scheme and general decorative plans came next. Our Norwegian table and chairs of unfinished pine occupy the center of the room. Mr. Kennedy designed the lighting and Paul and I chose the colors—white, blue green and green blue, with accents of natural wood and stove black.

Since we rejoice in the shapes of tools, cooking utensils became decorative objects, all carefully orchestrated by Paul, from pots and pot lids to skillets, trivets and flan rings. Even the knives are graduated according to shape and size, on vertical magnetic holders. Glass measures and earthenware pitchers are placed just so, while scissors hang in harmony with olive pitters, bottle openers and nutcrackers. We have a bookcase for dictionaries, atlases and bird lore, and paintings by friends. A painted artichoke lives over the wall ovens, and a painting of eggs hangs above the refrigerator—which also has a painted valentine glued to its door, along with Paul's colorful photographs of a *boeuf daube en gelée*, a *pâté en croûte* and a string of sausages.

Such was the initial design for the kitchen, and so it has remained, with minor changes, these many years. In it we receive our friends, we cook and dine, we teach and experiment. It is certainly the most loved and most used room in the house.

My own office opens off a second floor bedroom. By 1971 my television and writing projects had expanded to the point where I was bursting out of the little room. I needed space for my library and files and room enough to move around. Again we called on Robert Woods Kennedy, who extended the office by eliminating two adjoining walk-in closets.

We enjoy the rest of the house, too, of course. The large second floor bedroom serves Paul well as a studio, and he has one entire end of the basement for his workshop. In the basement also he has constructed two simple but workmanlike wine closets. The rest of the space offers ample room to store the television props I have accumulated.

We would never build a house like this. In the first place, who could afford one, let alone two, pantries nowadays? And I would never waste space on a dining room. We use ours frequently as a photographic studio; only occasionally for its original purpose. But after years of occupancy, ours is indeed a supremely comfortable home to cherish. Surrounded by good friends and large shade trees, we couldn't ask for a happier place to live.

LEFT: *The gray clapboard home of Paul and Julia Child "spoke" to the couple the first time they walked in the door. Surrounded by lush landscaping that includes pachysandra, ivy, laurel, rhododendron and impatiens, it needed only limited renovation to suit the entertaining and working needs of its owners.*

OPPOSITE ABOVE LEFT: *A tempera valentine painting done by Paul Child in the style of a Medieval stained glass panel greets visitors as they enter the house.*

OPPOSITE ABOVE RIGHT: *A Spanish refectory table in the Music Room supports favorite books and keepsakes.*

OPPOSITE: *Paul Child's painting* Marseilles Pastiche *lends a bold abstract quality to the grass-papered fireplace wall in the Music Room. Crowded bookshelves reveal the importance of books in the lives of the residents, while a blazing fire warms the informal atmosphere. A Spanish chair faces the hearth from its place on the floral hooked rug. Chamber music recitals are often held here, with Julia Child at the piano and her husband playing the violin. In the adjacent Entrance Hall a painting titled* Maine Rocks *rests on a handcarved walnut crédence. Both are the work of Paul Child.*

RIGHT: *Photographs and books personalize the Living Room. The subdued colors of Paul Child's* **French Village** *are complemented by the brightness of the fire and warm tones of the wood paneling. The asymmetrical low table serves as a display area for objets d'art, including a bronze statuette,* **Two Frightened Children,** *by Tovish; an antique pewter plate, French bronze mortar, Chinese bronze figurine and Portuguese pottery ashtray. A pair of bronze lions from the ancient Ceylonese city of Kandy guard the mantel.*

BELOW RIGHT: **Kunming Street Scene,** *a depiction of the Chinese city by Paul Child, complements the English mahogany double-pedestal Dining Room table. The backs of the French fruitwood chairs depict the* **Fables of La Fontaine.** *Julia Child admits that the dining room is often used "as a photographic studio; only occasionally for its original purpose." The couple prefer to serve guests in their favorite room, the kitchen.*

As might be expected, the Kitchen is considered the "center of the household." LEFT: *A collection of pots, pans and other cooking implements hangs decoratively on a pegboard-paneled wall. "We rejoice in the shapes of tools," says Julia Child.* BELOW: *The view of the Pantry from the Pastry Room is embellished by other colorful cooking tools. Copper casseroles line a high shelf, while a collection of wooden rolling pins seems to sprout from a pottery jar. A Dutch carved-wood cookie mold is suspended above an assortment of tinned-metal aspic, quiche and pâté molds.*

JONI MITCHELL

Living, to Joni Mitchell, is a contemplative expression of what she sees around her. A major force in the contemporary music world, her lyrics have become part of the social literature of our time. Her newly acquired house in Bel-Air, a secluded area of Los Angeles, needed to be her spirit defined in texture, color, line and shape.

"I thought a decorator would come in with lots of ideas, and suppress what I like," Miss Mitchell says. "My baskets and my Eskimo art, the way I like to live. Decorated rooms sometimes sacrifice feelings and emotions for the sake of chic. The look is sometimes *too* polished. I couldn't live in a house like that.

"A house is important to me. I have another place, in Canada, more like a cabin, really: one big room with a loft, and a cooking pot in the fireplace. There was no architect. I simply hired a stonemason, and we built it ourselves. The place itself is sheltered by trees that block out the view. Most city people would have cut them down and put in big glass windows. But if you want to see the view, you have to go outside. I like to go there three or four times a year and stay a couple of weeks—to feel renewed. I'm a nocturnal person, but I go to sleep there with the birds. I have good feelings in my house in California, too—the kind of feelings that go beyond the surface of *things.*"

Built in the 1920s, the house is in a luxuriant hilltop setting of flowers and shrubs; geraniums bloom in pots and Iceland poppies perch on stems that seem too fragile to hold their giant blossoms.

"When I bought the house it was run down," Joni Mitchell recalls. "There were inexpensive locks on the doors and lots of wire holding things together. There had been a lot of owners who didn't care; I had it repaired, then I began decorating it myself."

When Miss Mitchell didn't know what to do next, she went to Sally Sirkin Lewis, designer and owner of the J. Robert Scott showroom, and asked her advice. "But first," she adds, "I decided most things myself—like painting the bedroom walls white, and the dining room royal blue. The former owners had painted the molding across the ceiling in orange, yellow and turquoise stripes. When my business manager saw it he said, 'I think you need help.' So I asked Sally if she would come in."

Mrs. Lewis takes up the story. "After I saw the dining room, which was in the traditional colors of Italian donkey carts, I knew exactly the kind of house Joni wanted: colorful, charming, free. We started by sandblasting the dining room ceiling and painting the walls.

"Joni knew what she *didn't* want," says Mrs. Lewis, "which is more important than knowing what you do want. There are many approaches, many ways. She was open-minded and eager to consider new ideas. Her business manager was a little nervous at the beginning, but soon he told me to do anything I wanted. That was after the green wall incident."

Mrs. Lewis smiles enigmatically. "When I first saw Joni's bedroom," she goes on, "the walls were white, and the only furniture in it was her four-poster bed. The room looked like a bowling alley. I stared at it, and then suddenly I knew. 'Green,' I said, 'green walls.' Her business manager said, 'I've gone along with you so far, but green walls I resist.' Joni said, 'I want things pure and simple.' And I said, 'Forget pure and simple. Green walls. You'll have to trust me.' "

Today the bedroom is painted the color of a forest at dusk. Voluptuous ottomans, gently curved sofas and chairs—the same green as the walls—are grouped around the fireplace, and at hand are three guitars. It is one of Miss Mitchell's favorite areas of the house.

Mrs. Lewis, too, dislikes the "decorated" look. "All those fashion tricks. A house isn't a series of tricks," she remarks, "it's a reflection of a person—the essence of the one who lives there. The designer is responsible for interpreting personality. I don't believe in creating monuments for myself or my ego.

"Everything in design comes down to two people: the designer and the resident. That's all. It's so simple, and many designers complicate things with rules. You know, every lamp must be the same height, and every side table must be twenty-four inches high. Well, I say, Where is it written? Forget the games. Let's get down to basics and honesty. That's where design begins, and from there comes the sense of dramatic restraint, so important in every aspect of decorating."

The house is free from contrivance. It is glamorous, but humor is there as well—the black-and-white powder room, with its mirrored table, and vanity stool skirted in black taffeta and buttoned with a rosette, is reminiscent of the opulent 1940s.

On the walls are paintings by Miss Mitchell—the brooding words of her music swept into visual form on canvas. Fishtail palms, reaching nearly to the fourteen-foot ceiling, bend as if caught in the middle of a gale.

"At first I didn't know about this room," she says. "Before Sally came in, all I had in the living room was a small sofa in front of the fireplace. I would put on a record, and the space was like a ballroom. At night I would sprint through from my bedroom to the kitchen to make a snack. But when the new sofa came in, I thought it was choking up the space. You see, I'd lost my sense of proportion, because I'd never lived in such big rooms before. Now I'm happy here. It's my home."

ABOVE LEFT: *On the terrace, a stone lily pond, surrounded by desert plants, has a mellow sun-drenched look.*

ABOVE: *White wrought-iron gates and a deep stone archway form the entrance to Joni Mitchell's Spanish-style Bel-Air home, built in the 1920s. The terrace lily pond appears cool and welcoming beyond the Entrance Hall.*

OPPOSITE: *An overhanging loft gives a warm sheltered feeling to the corner of the Living Room where Miss Mitchell does most of her composing. A few leaves of New Zealand flax fall gracefully over the piano from a fishbowl-motif glass vase, and a richly embroidered Chinese robe drapes the bench. A large Navajo basket brings out the earthy colors of the terra-cotta floor tiles. The curving wrought-iron stairway leads to a book-lined loft with comfortable sofas and a writing desk.*

A lofty beamed ceiling in the Living Room accommodates twelve-foot fishtail palms, which have a windswept appearance. The soft velvet custom-designed sofa contrasts with abstract steel tables in front of the fireplace. An eighteenth-century ivory-inlaid box on a stand attends the sofa. Behind the sofa is a table covered in snakeskin. Tortoise shell, above the mantel, is a rare albino.

RIGHT: *Earth colors serve to establish a restful atmosphere in the simplified Dining Room. Candlelight from the wooden chandelier brings out specks of the original turquoise, yellow and orange paint on the coffered ceiling.*

Sleek modern surfaces and soft plush fabrics counterpoint the traditional architecture and terra-cotta flooring. Lucite chairs are suede-upholstered; side chairs are covered in striped velour. Indian artifacts line the eighteenth-century Welsh sideboard.

BELOW RIGHT: *Miss Mitchell's extensive collection of pre-Columbian and American Indian art personalizes her environment. Rare Navajo baskets fill a mirror-and-glass display niche.*

Miss Mitchell at first resisted designer Sally Sirkin Lewis's suggestion of forest green walls for the Master Bedroom, but today this dusky room is one of the owner's favorite areas in the house. Voluptuous mohair-wrapped chaise and chair are placed at dramatic angles in the large main portion of the room. The draped bronze four-poster bed, in an elevated alcove, is visually linked to the lower level by a boldly patterned carpet. Bronze-framed mirrors restate a pair of eighteenth-century cloisonné urns and a Tiffany floor lamp.

YVES SAINT LAURENT

The man and his work are contemporary—even avant-garde—yet the showcase of his fashion empire lies fast in the nineteenth century. With its opulent Second Empire décor, *La Maison Yves Saint Laurent,* housed in a private mansion on the avenue Montaigne, seems like some extravagant annex to the Paris Opera.

The designer's residence is redolent of still another period, the romantic twenties and early thirties. Situated on the Left Bank, the apartment is a few blocks from the Invalides, where Napoleon lies entombed. A duplex, it was originally designed by Jean-Michel Frank for an American woman who, unhappily, never lived there—her fortunes having declined dramatically on Wall Street in 1929. However, those who did occupy the building over the years kept almost everything intact. There are still Jean-Michel Frank touches everywhere, from the copper-edged window frames and door pulls to the radiator covers in molded black metal with linear grilles.

"You know," the designer says thoughtfully, "in France we don't have the same passion as in America, for harmonizing. This is because we have old rooms in old buildings that already have a personality. I have had to accept and then dramatize the 1920s décor that already existed. It's a mishmash, but still it's an expression of the times and, probably, a statement about myself. There's lots of brown and black, with touches of red, gold and bronze." The designer has an affinity for earth colors, particularly those of his native Algeria. "Color," he has said, "is a reflection of the soul."

Into this spare, almost modern, décor Yves Saint Laurent has put his own mixture of possessions: a collection of Art Déco furniture; whimsical pieces by his friends Claude and François-Xavier Lalanne; seventeenth- and eighteenth-century Italian bronzes; a sculpture by Alexander Liberman; here and there, ivory, shagreen and parchment tables. One corner of the living room is strewn with lamé pillows, presided over by a Siamese Buddha. Every room is graced by generous arrangements of his favorite flower the lily.

"Here is the best and the worst," he remarks casually. "Like life itself. After all, what is taste in a home? It is knowing when to stop and when to start again."

At his side, Hazel, the chubby Chihuahua, seems to nod in agreement, and Yves Saint Laurent looks thoughtfully around the large living room at his prized possessions. "All these things shimmer across the centuries," he remarks, running his hand with proprietary affection over the surface of a favorite bronze.

The ground floor of the apartment is less formal, less somber. It opens to a charming garden—bright and sunny, with a convent in the background. On this floor is the library, the couturier's favorite room, and a small study, both predominantly white and beige. Those colors the designer reserved for rooms to which he likes to retreat and work, a neutral background quickened by dashes of brilliant color. Characteristically they overflow with personal objects. There is a drawing by Modigliani, willed to the designer by Jean Cocteau; pictures of friends are everywhere; and a multitude of photographs of artists and actors and ballet dancers.

"These are the people I admire," he says. "Artists like Nureyev, Bakst, Plisetskaya and Diaghilev."

In fact one *prêt-à-porter* collection was inspired by the Ballet Russe. One of his early ambitions was to be the world's greatest theatrical designer, and in the past he has designed costumes for plays, films and ballets. He is unhappy that he has so little time for such work.

"You see, I'm writing a book now," he says in explanation. "I am planning it as a sort of inner dialogue with myself."

The subject is fascinating; perhaps the memoir will touch on some of the lesser-known aspects of an extraordinary life and career.

Ambitious to become a couturier, Saint Laurent went to Paris at seventeen, where, after a year of design school, he won first prize in a couture contest. This award led to a job with Christian Dior, and he collaborated with the great couturier for two years, until Dior's death. Left suddenly without its guiding force, the house asked Saint Laurent to design its upcoming collection, launching his career at twenty with the introduction of the "trapeze dress." Following a period in the French military, he left Dior and struck out on his own.

In the years since his first independent collection, in 1962, Saint Laurent and his business partner, Pierre Bergé, have built an enviable design empire reaching into every part of the world.

"I know my way now," says Yves Saint Laurent. "There is a theme and a continuity to my collections. Of course, there are always fantasies, but it is the base that counts. Elegance is in the heart, in the very being. It is really not a question of clothes at all."

Many of the same things can be said about his own apartment. It too is elegant. There is no other word. And in spite of his show of affection for the past—a Napoleon III showroom and an Art Déco apartment—the designer is very much a man of his own time and place.

Yves Saint Laurent has created a private world that expresses his artistic spirit in all its extraordinary facets.

"I have no nostalgia for the old days. I am glad that things change, and I suppose I can say that my success comes from being completely in harmony with my era."

In contrast to the Second Empire opulence of his Paris couture salon, the atmosphere of designer Yves Saint Laurent's duplex on the Left Bank is almost modern, and definitely a personal statement of refined eclecticism—with an emphasis on Art Déco. The apartment was originally designed by the late Jean-Michel Frank, whose crisp architectural lines and distinctive details enhance the sophisticated and elegant mélange.

LEFT: *In the front Entrance Hall a Greek torso of Alexander the Great, an eighteenth-century Chinese chair and a seventeenth-century Italian bronze head give a clue to the great variety of the collections.*

BELOW LEFT: *A Chippendale chair, one of a pair, and a Ptolemaic sarcophagus complement one another in the lower level Entrance Hall.*

A Manchu noble in a seventeenth-century Chinese silk painting
in the Living Room looks down upon an important collection of
furniture designed in the twenties and thirties, along with a
large number of sleek Renaissance bronzes. Tall Jean Dunand
vases flank the Jean-Michel Frank mirrored fireplace; other
Frank architectural details include copper-edged window frames
and molded metal radiator covers with copper grilles. Behind
the leather-upholstered Eileen Gray chair, whose serpent arms
are inlaid with ivory, is a 1635 statue of Mercury, by the
Flemish artist François Duquesnoy.

Further views of the Living Room reveal more of Yves Saint Laurent's comprehensive collection.

LEFT: Four square Pierre Chareau chairs face a sensual, naturalistic enamel panel by Dunand. The huge vases are also by Dunand, who became perhaps the leading exponent of metal and lacquer work of his time; his abstract geometric motifs were achieved with inlays of contrasting alloys. The low mirrored table supports a powerful Jean de Bologne bronze and a delicate Japanese ivory box. A small round shagreen table, by Dominique, holds a seventeenth-century bronze representing Bacchus, by Garnier, and a 1551 Limoges enamel coupe that once belonged to Diane de Poitiers. At the other side of the suede-covered Frank sofa is a table by Emile-Jacques Ruhlmann. A Pierre Legrain tabouret completes the luxurious setting.

ABOVE LEFT: An Albert Cheuret lamp on a Dunand table illuminates a fifteenth-century Flemish "cabbage leaves" tapestry. A bookcase below another Manchu noble displays a Dunand enamel of Josephine Baker and a bronze by Girardon representing the Rhine River. Serpent andirons and forged iron fireplace tools are by Edgar Brandt. "All these things shimmer across the centuries," says Saint Laurent.

ABOVE RIGHT: A tall Senufo totem perches in front of a luminous 1875 five-panel pastel by Sir Edward Burne-Jones, depicting The Two Rivers of Life; the cartoons originally were designs for windows of a Liverpool church.

While the upper level of the duplex is purposefully formal and
moodily somber, the lower level is white and flooded with
sunlight. Saint Laurent's favorite room, the Library, is here.
ABOVE: A flock of whimsical sheep chairs, sculptures by
Lalanne, share the room with other artworks, books and
photographs, all accentuated by a completely neutral
background. A Greek marble torso and an eighteenth-century
bronze head rest on pedestals near the bookshelves. Above a Le
Corbusier console are works by Léger, Picasso, Modigliani. The
alabaster-and-bronze table lamp is by Armand Rateau.
RIGHT: Andy Warhol's multiple images of Yves Saint Laurent
scan the room from above a bookcase. A Joseph Csaky
bas-relief, flanked by bronzes from the Ecole de Fontainebleau,
stands on the mirrored Frank mantel. The gleaming egg bar is
by Lalanne. Coiled on a mirrored table is a 1910 Art Nouveau
snake; others slither throughout the apartment—on vases and
andirons, consoles and chairs.

A small Study serves as a memory-filled retreat. Walls are covered with personal photographs, theatrical sketches, and works by Max Ernst, Christian Bérard and Jean-Louis Forain. The shagreen table by Dominique holds a René Lalique vase and a Cambodian dragon; the chair is by Jeanne Laurent. On the mantel is the elongated visage of an Assyrian statue.

Dark picture frames punctuate the room's pale tones. The Algerian-born fashion designer says he has "discovered color in Marrakech," referring to his house there. "It's very Somerset Maugham," he explains, "half Arabic, half English Colonial." Though he claims he can create anywhere, he escapes to Marrakech whenever he can: "There I empty my head and come back completely renewed."

The Music Room is an atmospheric medley.
ABOVE LEFT: *A cobra lamp by Brandt lights a Lalanne mirror, Ruhlmann chaise longue and lacquered Dunand chair.*
TOP: *Tall parchment-paned windows provide a dramatically contrasting geometric backdrop for a Ruhlmann piano and table. Chareau's cubist chairs rest on a vivid rug by Yvonne Loriot. The white sculpture on the piano is by Laurens.*
ABOVE: *Dunand's shapely vases are artfully arranged on the piano; lacquered fish figurines seem to float in the darkness.*

DOLORES DEL RIO

"I wanted a very Mexican house," says Dolores Del Rio, recalling the day over three decades ago when she chose her home in Mexico City.

"One afternoon my mother and I were shown this place. We came through the heavy doors from the street and saw the garden and the lovely trees. I turned to my mother and said, 'This is it!'

"The real estate woman showing us the place said, 'Fine. I'm glad you like it. Now let's go in, and I'll show you the house.' I replied, 'No, I'm not going in. If I don't like the interiors, I might not buy it. Then I'll be without this garden, and that's a chance I'm certainly not going to take.' I bought the house the next day and then I was frightened. I thought, 'What on earth have I done?'"

She might have been more frightened had she known about the ghost. Some time later she was told of the spirit, El Charro de Coyoacán, whose existence, according to Miss Del Rio, has been documented in at least two histories of the area.

"All of this was once part of an hacienda called *La Escondida*," she explains. "Some of the thick walls were built during the last century. According to legend, when the hacienda was destroyed the charro lost his ladylove. Now he returns, searching for her, at midnight when the moon is full." Ghost or no ghost, Dolores Del Rio and her producer/director husband, Lewis A. Riley, reside happily in their hacienda, hidden behind high walls, in the select Mexico City suburb of Coyoacán.

"The reason for coming to Mexico was type-casting," explains Mr. Riley. "Hollywood couldn't think of Dolores Del Rio as anything except a Spanish madonna, a Mexican señorita or an Indian squaw. In Mexico, Dolores had her choice of roles and directors."

"During my first years in Hollywood," Miss Del Rio recounts, "I was doing five and six films a year. We just turned them out like that." She snaps her fingers. "Some of those films were very bad, but I think some of them were very good. Some are in the Museum of Modern Art in New York, and in official collections in Moscow and London and Paris—so they *must* have been good."

The move to Mexico definitely enhanced the star's career. She has returned frequently to make films in Hollywood, not cast to a particular type but as an actress of international reputation. In Mexico she has been able to devote more time to the legitimate theater, an interest for which she had little time in her Hollywood years.

The move to Mexico also created problems. The most immediate of these was the house she had bought, sight unseen. "It was very old-fashioned," she recalls. "It had high ceilings and heavy beams. I don't like high ceilings, so they had to be lowered." Miss Del Rio called in Robert Block, a Paris-based interior designer who had recently established an office in Mexico.

"Really," she says, "it was Robert Block who did the house. He tried to give it a very modern and Mexican feeling because that is what I wanted—because that is what I am—Mexican and modern."

Mr. Block not only lowered the ceilings but added contemporary regional touches. He ordered designs with typical Mexican styling—cacti are painted on the mantel of the living room fireplace and tropical fruit enhances a gold *petate* beneath the glass of the dining room table.

For a movie star of legendary beauty, he placed floor-to-ceiling mirrors everywhere: in the foyer, in the boudoir, between her bedroom and the library.

As different as the roles she portrays are the numerous canvases of Dolores Del Rio as she appeared to John Carroll, Adolfo Best, Roberto Montenegro, Rosa Covarrubias, Miguel Covarrubias, José Clemente Orozco and Diego Rivera. But other hints that this is the home of a motion picture star are few.

Traditional yet individualistic, the house speaks eloquently of the couple living within. The first floor living room and dining room, reserved for formal entertaining, still evoke a feeling of the early 1940s. Upstairs, on the second floor, the house becomes more personal. Here the owners are revealed as enthusiastic collectors of pre-Columbian art, and as avid readers as well. The large and varied collection of pre-Columbian statues and artifacts are vivid reminders of Mexico's past. There are delicate figures from the funeral island of Jaina on a low table in Miss Del Rio's bedroom. Idols from Colima and Nayarit stand guard in Mr. Riley's bedroom and study.

"Dolores and I each had pre-Columbian collections when we were married, in 1960," Mr. Riley remarks. "It's been so many years now, we've completely forgotten who originally owned what."

Mr. Riley's private study is lined with well-thumbed books, as is the library the two share as an intimate upstairs living room. Here, curled in comfortable armchairs, they often take their evening meals on trays.

But they are most at home in the magnificent gardens they both love. Miss Del Rio sometimes breakfasts while strolling in the garden, carrying a plate of papaya and looking up at the towering eucalyptus, elm, jacaranda, banana and rubber trees. There is a zestful mix of formal box hedges, yucca and delicate tree ferns. Bright blossoms of hydrangea, bougainvillea, magnolia and *Rosa Mexicana* compete for attention.

Massive Spanish Colonial gates frame a final view of the enchanting garden that first captivated Dolores Del Rio many years ago.

This is the view of **La Escondida** that sold Dolores Del Rio on the property when she first visited it, more than three decades ago. The actress fell in love with the lush gardens surrounding the house on the former hacienda and bought it immediately, without even seeing the interior.

Miss Del Rio moved into the residence, located in the select Mexico City suburb of Coyoacán, when she returned to her native land in 1943 to escape being type-cast in Hollywood. In Mexico and internationally her career has flourished on screen and stage for more than half a century.

Robert Block, the Paris-based interior designer, modernized the main house and enhanced the Mexican feeling the actress cherishes. Miss Del Rio and her husband, producer/director Lewis A. Riley, continue to share La Escondida with a well-documented ghost—a charro who searches for his lost ladylove at midnight during a full moon.

OPPOSITE: *Mr. Riley brought this pre-Columbian stone artifact with Olmec characteristics from the southwest Mexican state of Guerrero to the gardens of La Escondida.*

OPPOSITE BELOW: *A café table setting awaits the Rileys on a glistening Terrace just washed by an early-morning tropical shower. The chairs, typically Mexican in design, are covered in pigskin. A path lined with shaped hedges leads to the main entrance, which is marked by a massive stone-and-wood Spanish Colonial gateway set into the high walls that border the secluded property. The name of the estate is set into fired tiles near the gateway.*

ABOVE LEFT: *The Living Room, used primarily for entertaining, still has the same early-1940s flavor it had when it was first designed. To add a Mexican touch, cacti were painted on the mirrored mantel above the streamline-design fireplace. The ceiling was lowered, to modernize the setting. The dramatic portrait of Miss Del Rio was painted by John Carroll in 1943.*

ABOVE: *In one corner of the Living Room, Oriental objects are arranged before the panorama of a seventeenth-century Coromandel screen.*

LEFT: *The soft glow of tall tapers illuminates a 1943-44 Diego Rivera portrait of the international film star, and the Dining Room table set with antique Mexican silver. The high-backed chairs have a scalloped shell motif.*

Dolores Del Rio and Lew Riley merged their extensive individual collections of pre-Columbian art when they married—filling the residence with the exuberant sculpture.

OPPOSITE ABOVE: *A back-bending acrobat from the southwest Mexican state of Colima encounters himself in a mirrored Library tabletop.*

ABOVE: *The Library is a large, informal much-used room. Shelves are filled to overflowing with old and new books, punctuated by pre-Columbian figures. The Rileys often relax in the fireside chairs in the evening and discuss the day's events over dinner on trays.*

LEFT: *A seated Olmec figure weeps among cheery-visaged Remojadas figures in a Hallway niche. This hallway, which connects Miss Del Rio's bedroom and the library, features floor-to-ceiling mirrors.*

Another view of the residence is framed by luxuriant foliage in the gardens of La Escondida. The Rileys take pleasure in strolling the verdant grounds, enjoying the splashes of color from bright blooms of hydrangea, bougainvillea, magnolia and Rosa Mexicana. *A thriving variety of trees includes eucalyptus, elm, jacaranda, banana and rubber. And dotted throughout the carefully tended greenery are stone figures and pre-Columbian statues to delight the eye and the imagination.*

CREDITS

PHOTOGRAPHERS

Jaime Ardiles-Arce *196—203*

Cecil Beaton *34—41*

Jeremiah O. Bragstad *120—129, 130—137, 138—143*

Robert Emmett Bright *144—151*

Allen Carter *242—251*

Richard Champion *112—119, 152—157, 158—163, 172—181, 182—189, 204—209, 218—223, 224—231*

Max Eckert *12—23, 24—33, 50—57, 88—97*

Pascal Hinous *232—241*

Leland Lee *42—49, 74—79*

Russell MacMasters *210—217*

Greg Molesworth *58—63*

Derry Moore *98—105*

Edward Pfizenmaier *80—87*

F. Wayne Stellmacher *164—171*

George R. Szanik *106—111*

Fritz Taggart *190—195*

WRITERS

The following writers prepared the original *Architectural Digest* articles from which the material in this book has been adapted:

Susan Heller Anderson
Helen Barnes
Reva Berger
Mary Blume
Sam Burchell
Peter Carlsen
Allen Carter
Julia Child
Jane Geniesse
Dick Hobson
Rosemary Kent
Jean Kerr
Valentine Lawford
Russell MacMasters
Suzanne Stark Morrow
Andrea Levinger Smith

ACKNOWLEDGMENTS

At *Architectural Digest* we often say "people are the issue." That is certainly true of our first book, CELEBRITY HOMES.

Many staff members and associates of *Architectural Digest* magazine were involved in adapting the original material to produce this book, and we appreciate their efforts equally, although we will thank those who were most involved alphabetically:

EVERETT T. ALCAN, Controller, Knapp Communications Corporation.

ALICE BANDY, Administrative Assistant, The Knapp Press.

SUSAN BERNARD, *Architectural Digest* Features Editor.

JANE JORDAN BROWNE, who rewrote and edited the original text.

RICHARD BYE, Managing Director of The Knapp Press, who planned and implemented the marketing of CELEBRITY HOMES, the first of a number of books to be published by The Knapp Press.

GARRY JAMES, Knapp Press Associate Editor.

PHILIP KAPLAN, Graphics Director of *Architectural Digest* and The Knapp Press, who designed the format and supervised all graphics.

BRUCE KORTEBEIN, Design Consultant.

JOHN LINCOLN, *Architectural Digest* Antiques Consultant.

CHRISTOPHER PHILLIPS, of the *Architectural Digest* editorial staff.

HENRY RATZ, Production Director.

MARGARET REDFIELD, *Architectural Digest* Copy Editor.

GAYLE MOSS ROSENBERG, *Architectural Digest* Caption Writer.

STUART H. SALSBURY, *Architectural Digest* Art Consultant.

DAVID W. STEADMAN, *Architectural Digest* Art Consultant.